*Walk up!*
*Walk up!*
*Walk up!*

*This way for one of the
most singular stories ever
told by living man!*

First published in London 1910

This Muddler Books edition published 2018
Introduction © 2018 by Matthew Crampton

ISBN 978-0-9561361-4-5

Designed by Matthew Crampton

Illustrations in this edition come from the collections of
Matthew Crampton and John Foreman. They include works by
George Cruikshank, Thomas Bewick and others.

muddlerbooks.com
matthewcrampton.com

# SEVENTY YEARS A SHOWMAN

'Lord' George Sanger

Muddler Books

# CONTENTS

# INTRODUCTION by Matthew Crampton

DANCING off the page like real-life Dickens, this legendary autobiography of Victorian circus pioneer 'Lord' George Sanger is dark, fun and irresistible. As befits a man who lived by his wits, he tells a great story. When he produced this book in 1910, then in his eighties, Sanger had spent decades honing tales from a life of rare breadth and bravery.

Most people today know of the American showman P. T. Barnum, but few, even in Britain, have heard of 'Lord' George Sanger. That's odd, for Sanger was then as famous in Europe. He was also the American's equal in skill, pluck and cheek. But while Barnum's story is often sanitised, this book is not. It's as rooted in the darkness as the spectacle of both men's lives.

First we meet Sanger's father James as a teenage farmer from Wiltshire, visiting London to see pals. Crossing London Bridge, he is waylaid by a press gang, which bludgeons him into service on a government ship. He ends up aboard the flagship *Victory* during the Battle of Trafalgar, survives boarding an enemy ship, and watches Nelson fall. James returns home, maimed and poor, but is badly received by his family. So he sets out on the road, to live by means of a peep-show and patter. All this, and we're barely four pages into the book.

Such paternal setback steers the life of our hero. After Trafalgar, his father was given a piece of paper – a royal prescription – letting him carry on any honest trade, travel freely and be exempted from some laws. Rejected by his family, he now had both incentive and licence to go and do as he wished. Young George was born in 1827 and grew up in a caravan. Every few nights the family slept somewhere new. By the age of six, he was already declaiming recent murders to spellbound audiences.

The family had to fend for itself. When George's younger sister caught smallpox in Newbury, father fashioned a vaccination for the other children. *His instrument was a long darning-needle. This he passed through the upper part of the muscle of each child's right arm. Then into the tiny wound on each side he rubbed a little of the serum taken from the pustules of the sufferer.* Amazingly, it worked. Later, when young

George's leg was ripped apart on stage, and two doctors said it must be amputated, his father operated himself with a needle and silk thread. *I did my best not to whimper, though I was very glad when I saw him put that big curved needle down.* The leg healed.

Like his father, George felt licensed to go and do as he pleased. He soon set up his own show, along with brothers William and John. In time, this entrepreneurial urge saw him pioneer spectacular circus decades before Barnum & Bailey arrived in Britain, launch the first Lord Mayor's Parade in London and tour Europe with a huge cast of performers and animals.

After opening his first circus in the 1854, Sanger's rise was relentless. By 1871 he'd bought Britain's largest permanent circus, Astley's in London, while also running shows in Islington, Manchester, Birmingham and eight other cities. One spectacle alone gathered on stage 300 women, 200 men, 200 children, 13 elephants, 9 camels, and 52 horses, in addition to ostriches, emus, pelicans, deer, kangaroos, buffaloes, bulls and – at the centre of it all – two African lions.

There's a delicious danger to circus life, which this book lets you taste fully. When a fight breaks out between rival shows on the road, *Even the freaks took part. The fat man made for the living skeleton with a door-hook; the living skeleton battered at the fat man with a peg mallet.* One typically picaresque scene finds performers uniting to tackle a factory fire near Stepney Fair. *Amid the flying sparks ... could be seen clowns, knights in armour, Indian chiefs, jugglers in tights and spangles, rope-walkers in fleshings.* The tight-rope walkers prove useful in clambering along high beams to contain the fire's advance through the roof.

Circus folk are a breed apart. In a wonderful commentary on this book by *Wind in the Willows* author Kenneth Grahame (included at the back of this edition), we read: *Show-people are a contented folk ... because they rarely want to be anything but what they are. They are a quiet and reserved people, subdued in manner, clannish, living a life apart; scrupulously clean and tidy, as indeed anyone must be who lives in a caravan; self-reliant, asking little from anyone except some tolerance from officials and freedom to come and go.*

Sanger repeatedly rose from setbacks which might sink others. For Christmas 1850 he risked all on pantomimes in central London, but the theatre he rented was found to be built over a hundred barrels of human remains – it was a makeshift graveyard – so he had to beat a costly retreat. Two years later in Northwich, just as the family were preparing to perform, their carriage was destroyed by a gas explosion, injuring him and his pregnant wife Nellie. Then, while being treated, their savings were stolen from the wreckage. They were offered compensation, which Sanger proudly refused, quoting his father: *Never eat the bread of charity if you can avoid it.* Adapted to their injuries, the show went on, Sanger conjuring, while his wife *took on the second-sight business.* They played to capacity audiences, earning twelve pounds a house.

Life was always hard. Shortly after the explosion, Nellie gave birth, George's mother came north to see the grandchild, but died suddenly in Durham. There was barely time to bury her before they had to travel on – they needed the money – and misfortunes escalated until they reached Lincolnshire, in mid-winter, where their new baby died. To pay for the funeral, they kept playing. *In the bitter grey weather, our hearts as heavy as lead, we had to mount jests and smile to win the people to our show.*

Forgive a second titanic namedrop, but Sanger is near Shakespearean in his voyage through the classes and geographies of his time. One minute he's bare-knuckle fighting in an East End pub, the next entertaining toffs on the Isle of Wight. He claimed to have performed to every community in Britain of more than 100 inhabitants. And whether he was recruiting a fake tribe of red Indians from Liverpool slums, dodging the fury of a Chartist riot or chatting with Queen Victoria about elephants, Sanger remained resolutely the same man.

And what a man that was. Clad in glossy top hat, frock coat and boots, he was a spritely showman who prized action over paperwork. While he was able to read, it's likely he could not write, and this book was probably ghosted by the journalist George R. Sims. Sanger grew up in a world where the law offered little security against local citizens or authorities, both of which took pleasure in attacking travelling showfolk. So Sanger trusted few outside his world. *Within* his world, however, he exerted control by force of personality and by promoting a near-cult of circus 'family', of which he, naturally, was head.

Sanger's grandson – also called George, also a showman – wrote much about the grandfather in his own 1950s autobiography. This book *The Sanger Story* provides useful counterpoint to the mythology of *Seventy Years a Showman.* While 'Lord' George presents himself as a benign, loving leader, grandson George portrays a fault-finding grump, never satisfied, for example, with how his bacon was cooked. More insight comes from great-great-grandson, also George Sanger, who appeared on BBC radio's *Desert Island Discs* in 1962. Asked about the original 'Lord' George, he says, "I was frightened to death of him."

No-one builds an empire without knocking a few heads along the way. In Sanger's case, literally. Though light in tone, the early chapters reveal a world of constant violence. The showfolk are often ambushed by aggressive townsfolk. Toddler George nearly dies when their caravan is overturned by a mob. Chapters Nine and Ten are a glorious account of the dangers of performing near Bath, whose riotous roughs are led by *a red-headed virago, a dreadful giantess of a woman, known as "Carroty Kate"*; Sanger relishes the revenge taken by the circus workers. *A brutal sight, you may say; but, oh, the excitement of it!* Later, at the Stalybridge Wakes, he sees a gang of Lancastrians kick a stallholder to death with their iron-tipped clogs.

This was a business built upon deception. At its heart was the skill of 'hanky-panky' – a term now smutty, but then referring to the arts of conjuring, juggling and patter. As with magic, audiences were happy to be deceived. And 'Lord' George gleefully shares his secrets. For his *Shoal of Trained Fish in their Exhibition of a Naval Engagement*, he got goldfish to steer model boats armed with small explosives. He presented an oyster who appeared to enjoy smoking a pipe. There were fortune-telling ponies. *The Pig-faced Lady* was actually a bear. All good fun.

But around them at the fairs were less noble deceptions, which Sanger is just as happy to recount. Chapter 24 gives fascinating insight into 'tog-tables' – false gambling tables which paid out big to 'bonnets' (planted audience members), but never let the real public win. Sanger does admit to some guilty feelings. Describing his fake red Indians – publicised as having to be housed in an iron-barred carriage to contain their savagery – he says *My! It was a swindle, and now and again my conscience troubled me fearfully about it.*

Of the many skills of the circus performer, training and working with animals was crucial. *Never lose your temper with an animal,* explains 'Lord' George. *You can without any unkind treatment teach him to do anything you want him to do.* His wife Nellie had been known as the Lion Queen at rival Wombwell's Menagerie (no doubt useful knowledge for coping with her husband's temperament); soon after she joined Sanger, her cousin Miss Bright was mauled to death by a tiger with whom she had often performed. *I have never known a wild beast kill a keeper or trainer unless the animal has been previously ill-used or tormented*, says Sanger. Here, Miss Bright had foolishly flicked her whip around the tiger's eyes. 'Lord' George adored his beasts. When a favourite old lion caught pneumonia, he spent all night beside it in the den, rubbing mustard through the fur onto its chest.

Sanger's love of animals was matched by his love of royalty. He would do anything to please Queen Victoria, even rushing the entire circus to Balmoral when Her Majesty expressed interest. Such royal attachments were, of course, good for business, and widely publicised, but Sanger did bow to Saxe-Coburgs in ways he could not for other humans. He even found himself unable to lie to them. When the Prince of Wales asked whether *The only White Elephant ever seen in the Western World* was the real thing, he said *I could never deceive my future king* and admitted it was an ordinary elephant given a twice-daily coat of whitewash. *My goodness, how the Prince did laugh!*

Before letting you loose on this marvellous book, two more matters need explanation. First, Sanger was a 'Lord' of his own promotion. When Buffalo Bill Cody brought his Wild West show across the Atlantic in 1887, he wasn't happy to find Sanger already touring his own 'Scenes from Buffalo Bill', and took him to court. Hearing his rival titled the 'Honourable William Cody', Sanger angrily declared that he would forthwith be known as 'Lord' George. The name stuck. It's said, indeed, that Sanger thrice turned down offers of knighthood from Queen Victoria, for this would mean giving up being a 'Lord'.

Finally, there is the matter of his death. Unsurprisingly absent from his autobiography, the story is so strange and violent, it's fitting to mention. In November 1911, Sanger was attacked at his Finchley home by disgruntled employee Herbert Cooper, first with a hatchet, then with a brass vase. He died of his injuries. Cooper jumped under a train at Crouch End. The murder caused headlines around the world. It was a departure as sensational as his life.

Now, sit back, start reading – and get ready to be amazed.

# AUTHOR'S PREFACE

SEVENTY years a showman. Seventy years!

A long, long day is waning at last. Here in the peaceful shadows of the Garden of Life I pause awhile. I want to drink in the scene. I want to realize the full meaning of it all.

Rest – yes, I can rest now. The way has been long. It has often been weary. A showman's life, my friends, isn't all glory. Beneath the glitter and the tinsel is many a heartache. The open road is often strewn with thorns.

And now the journey is nearly ended. Far away in the west I see the setting sun. The garden is hushed in sleep. Ay! The showman's day is gone. The shutters are up. The camp fire, long lighted, is dying away. In its glowing embers I see strange faces. They are the faces of the Past.

Tell us the showman's tale, you say. And why not? The very thought of it brings back to my ears the jingle of bells. The dim figures before me turn into a thousand shapes and fancies. Tell you the showman's tale? Ay, that I will. Once more I hear the blare of music and the sound of drums. I catch the laughter of merry children.

Walk up! Walk up! Walk up!

This way for one of the most singular stories ever told by living man!

This way for a tale of strange things, scenes, and adventures!

Bang! bang! Bang! goes the old drum: and Lord George Sanger is on the road again!

From John o' Groats to Penzance – ay, further, even to the little rock-set town of St. Just – I have travelled this land of ours as a showman some scores of times in the last seventy years. In that period I have seen my show grow from a modest box on wheels to the biggest combination of circus and menagerie this country has ever produced.

There is not, I believe, a town or village of over one hundred inhabitants in this United Kingdom I have not at some time or other visited. So, too, abroad. With the exception of Russia, I have carried my tents into every European country.

I shall carry you with me back to the days of my boyhood, when the conditions of life for all classes of workers, and for show-folk in particular, were harsh and hard to a degree unknown to the present generation. You shall be shown how the peep-show carried in a box on the back of the showman grew into a wagon, and the wagon into many caravans and a great combination.

I shall show you what cunning tricks and artifices were resorted to in the early days to draw the pennies from the pockets of the crowds that thronged the old fairs, many of which are now but names and memories. You will witness the fierce rivalries of the showmen of those times and the fights and riots that arose in consequence.

I shall take you with me behind the scenes and show you how beasts are trained and tamed. I shall tell you how pigs become learned and ponies are taught to prophesy and tell fortunes. You shall learn the secrets of the horse-breakers, and see how the most vicious steeds are transformed into equine marvels of docility and intelligence.

On my travels you shall go with me into the company of the highest and the lowest. It has been my fortune to mix with all sorts and conditions of men. Angry mobs have stormed my tents and more than once gone far to wreck what little fortune I had got together by months and years of toil and patience. On the other hand, I have had great triumphs, such, I believe, without undue boasting, as have fallen to the lot of no other showman in the world.

Our present gracious King and Queen and the late Queen Victoria have honoured me many times with commands and gifts. The Prince and Princess of Wales and other members of our Royal Family have also done me kindnesses, for which I have no words to express my gratitude.

Abroad it has been my good fortune to meet with the personally expressed approval of their Imperial Majesties the German Emperor and the Emperor of Austria. In earlier days the Emperor Napoleon III and the Empress Eugenie were amongst my patrons. In Rome I received the unique honour of two visits from His Holiness Pope Pius IX.

When in America many years ago I saw and conversed with Abraham Lincoln, the most famous President the United States has ever had. There is also the memory of a visit paid to my establishment – then a very small one indeed – by the Czar, Nicholas I, when he was in England as the guest of Queen Victoria.

What these great personages had to say to the showman you will learn in the course of this story of my life. I have written it not without hope that I may succeed in once more interesting and amusing that great public which, throughout my long career, has proved my staunchest and most generous friend.

# CHAPTER I

## MY PARENTS AND EARLY DAYS

I COME of a good old Wiltshire stock, my father, James Sanger, being the youngest son of a well-to-do farmer who tilled a goodly number of acres in the village of Tisbury, on the edge of Salisbury Plain. After a course of what was then considered most excellent schooling, but which in these days would fill the most lenient education authority with pious horror, my parent was apprenticed to an edged toolmaker in Salisbury, and was expected in the intervals of learning his trade to follow the plough and otherwise assist in the work of a small farm possessed by his master.

Possibly this early variation of employment was the foundation of that adaptability to circumstances and readiness of resource which were marked traits in my father's character, and proved of such value to him in the career he was ultimately to take up. In any case, he steadily pursued this mixed business of farming and tool-making until his eighteenth year, when another change of the most unforeseen and sweeping character came suddenly into his life.

He had some friends in London whom he used to visit at long intervals, the time and expense of the journey in those days making it impossible for him to see them very often. He had been looking forward to one of these visits for some time when his eighteenth birthday arrived, and his master allowed him to celebrate it with a fortnight's holiday. Accordingly, he tied the money he had been saving for the event into his handkerchief, put on his best suit, and took the wagon for the Metropolis. That was the last his relatives, friends, and master saw of him for ten long years.

The reason, only learned at the expiration of this period, was that he had been trapped into serving his country. After leaving the wagon in which he arrived in London he made his way towards the house of his friends. The road lay over London Bridge, and when he was half across that famous structure he suddenly saw a great commotion amongst the passing crowd, and heard loud cries of "Press! Press!"

Before he could realize what was happening, he was seized by several stalwart men-o'-war's men, and despite his protests and a vigorous use of his fists, with which he was very handy, he found himself an hour later on the Government tender in the Thames, near Deptford, with some 150 groaning and complaining fellow-sufferers gathered up by the pressgangs to fight Britannia's battles on the sea.

A few days after being pressed he was, with some companion captives, taken from the tender to Deal, and transferred to the *Agincourt*, which lay in the Downs with other vessels of the Fleet, and there he learned his duties as a sailor. In the *Agincourt* he witnessed a terrible storm in the Bay of Biscay, and saw two vessels go down, it being impossible to render them any aid. After seeing much service off the coast of France he was eventually transferred to the *Pompey*, and the latter vessel, returning with despatches, brought up in the Downs, where another incident occurred, which also had its effect on my father's after life.

From shore many bumboats were allowed to come off for the purpose of trafficking with the tars, and on one boat two venturesome passengers in the persons of two Jews, brothers, named Israel and Benjamin Hart, were brought to the *Pompey*, and came on deck. The brothers were strolling conjurers, who in their travels had happed on Deal, and, seeing the vessel in the Downs, thought there was an opportunity of turning an honest penny by displaying their skill to the sailors. But the idea was their undoing, for, discovering that they were able-seamen, the captain seized them for the service of the King.

Curiously enough, the Harts made very good sailors and brave fighting men, but with that I have here nothing to do. My chief interest in the story lies in the fact that, in return for various kindnesses, they taught my father many conjuring and hanky-panky tricks that stood him, and incidentally myself, in good stead in later years.

After various adventures my father was eventually transferred to Nelson's flagship the *Victory*, served on her at the Battle of Trafalgar, and saw the hero fall. Nor did he escape unscathed. He was one of twenty-six men who, in the very height of the battle, boarded a vessel of the enemy, eleven of his companions being cut down. He sustained a severe scalp wound, lost several fingers, and had some of his ribs broken. On the return of the Fleet he was paid off at Deal with other invalids, and received the magnificent pension of £10 a year from his grateful country.

His first thought on arriving in England was to visit his family, and he at once went into Wiltshire. His reception, however, was the reverse of cordial. During his ten years' absence from home his parents had died, and his brothers, of whom he had four – one a King's waterman, one a dissenting minister in Salisbury, another a chemist, and the fourth a pleader in the Old Court of Arches at Exeter House – intimated that his return as a maimed, poor sailor was anything but welcome to them. The hint was quite enough for my father. After a little plain speaking, the faculty for which, amongst other accomplishments, he had acquired in his seafaring life, he bade them a curt adieu, and went to seek a living as best he could.

Happening to go to Bristol fair, and remembering what the two Harts had taught him in the way of hanky-panky and conjuring, he resolved to be a showman, and as a start invested what money he had got in the purchase and fitting up of a small peep show. This was nothing more than a large box carried on the back, containing some movable and very gaudy pictures, and having six peep-holes fitted with fairly strong lenses. When a pitch was made, the box was placed on a folding trestle and the public were invited to walk up and see the show.

My father was an excellent talker. He could "patter" in the most approved style, especially about the Battle of Trafalgar, scenes of which formed one of the staple features of his little show. In his white smock-frock, beaver hat, knee-breeches, with worsted stockings and low-buckled shoes – a costume, by the way, he never varied till the day of his death – the tall, handsome, well-set-up young fellow attracted much attention in the fair then held in the Churchyard, which now forms the Haymarket, Bristol. Amongst others drawn to look at him and see his show was a young lady named Elliott, whom he had known as a child, and who was then a lady's maid in Bristol. Their acquaintance was joyfully renewed, and, after a short courtship, they were married at Bedminster, my mother's native town. Thus it was my father got one of the best wives a man was ever blessed with, and the children who eventually made their appearance the dearest and kindest of mothers. Her own mother at that time kept a large house known as the "Black Horse" at Bedminster.

# CHAPTER II

## SECRETS OF THE FREAK SHOW

FATHER was in every way a "handy man," and soon got together materials for his first caravan, with which he and mother could travel the country. This caravan had its rod and sides made of thin sheets of iron, and was far from comfortable. My mother has told me that in the summer it was baking hot and in the winter terribly cold, so that as a rule they preferred to camp in a tent which they carried as part of the show.

In regard to the latter my father had ambitions. He procured new pictures, and made a bigger peep show, and resolved on additional attractions in the way of living curiosities. To obtain these was the difficulty; but equal to the occasion, and very soon was travelling with "Madame Gomez, the tallest woman in the world," and "Tamee Ahmee and Orio Rio, the savage cannibal pigmies of the Dark Continent."

The descriptions sound very imposing, but those "living curiosities" were not all they seemed. My father had taken a showman's licence in introducing these novelties to the public. This often involves a judicious economy of the truth, and as I have promised to tell how these things are done I will proceed to explain.

First as to Madame Gomez. She had nothing foreign about her but the name, nor was she very remarkable as a giantess. Art, however, aids where nature stops short, and this is where my father came in. Madame was exhibited on a raised platform in the travelling booth, and when the company was assembled the curtains were pulled aside, and she stepped forward from a mass of draperies at the back. Her actual height, which might have been nearly six feet, was added to by her high heels and cork raisers in her shoes, and – note the point – her dresses were made very full and long.

Seen from the floor she certainly looked very tall, and my father would "patter" to the audience in this style: "This, ladies and gentlemen, is Madame Gomez, admitted to be the tallest woman the world has ever seen. So admirably, however, is she proportioned that her great height does not immediately impress the observer. In order, therefore, to assure you that there is no deception, I will ask the tallest gentleman in the company to ascend the platform. You will then see that he has not the slightest difficulty in passing under Madame's extended arm."

The tallest man would soon be picked out, and as he ascended the steps to the small platform Madame would pull her long dress aside, and draw backwards as if to make room. In making this movement she imperceptibly gained a little step or dais, cunningly concealed by the back draperies. This dais added at least seven inches to her height; while the long dress fell round her in seemingly perfect fit. The arm test was, of course, always easily passed under these conditions, and the spectators invariably went away satisfied that there was "no deception."

So, also, there was a similar little juggling with the truth in regard to Tamee Ahmee and Orio Rio, the "savage cannibal pigmies." They were really two rather intelligent mulatto children, their mother being a negress and their father an Irishman. My father had got them from their mother in Bristol, and they were aged respectively ten years and nine years. Feathers, beads, and carefully applied paint gave them the necessary savage appearance, and the "patter" did the rest.

"Ladies and Gentlemen: These wonderful people are fully grown, being, in fact, each over thirty years of age. They were captured by Portuguese traders in the African wilds, and are incapable of ordinary human speech. Their food consists of raw meat, and if they can capture a small animal they tear it to pieces alive with their teeth, eagerly devouring its flesh and drinking its blood."

Thus was the tale told, and the credulous country folks were mightily impressed. So successful, indeed, was the whole show that rivals on the road hated my father bitterly, complaining that when he was about he took all the money. This enmity bore very bitter fruit a little later on at Taunton in Devon, where the show had been doing unusually good business.

Somebody laid information before the authorities there that the cannibals and the giantess were impostors, and that my father was gaining his living by deceiving the public. For this offence proceedings could be taken under a now obsolete statute, and there was an order issued for the arrest of the proprietor of the show – namely, my father. As it happened, however, the beadle of Taunton was my father's first cousin, and he gave a timely intimation of what was afoot. My father, desirous of keeping out of the clutches of the law, which at that period sternly dealt with the showfolk as "rogues and vagabonds," whenever it had the chance, considered that flight was his best possible course, more particularly as with him out of the road the authorities could not interfere with his wife.

He accordingly mounted one of the two horses he possessed, and rode away as fast as he could, eventually reaching his native place of Tisbury, in Wiltshire. Here he stayed until he was joined by my mother after the show had been broken up, and the two "cannibals" removed to Bristol Workhouse. Both did very well in later life, and I saw the pair on several occasions, when they paid visits to our show. After the break-up of the show, and my mother had joined him at Tisbury, father looked about for something to turn his hand to, as he had now a small family, and eventually went to Trowbridge, where he opened a small general shop. He was in Trowbridge about two years, but though he did fairly well he did not like the town, and, moreover, was restless for the road again. So he gave up the shop and moved on to Newbury, in Berkshire, a place he always had a liking for, and here it was that I made my appearance in the world.

There is a legend that has grown up, though how it originated I cannot tell, that I and my brother, John Sanger, were twins, and that we were born in Newbury Workhouse. Also that in that institution I received the baptismal name of Lord George. Now, I like innocent fairy-tales, and am the last man on earth to desire to spoil a good story, especially if it redounds to one's credit, as this is supposed to do, for it is a much harder thing to get out of a workhouse and acquire a position than it is to lose a position and get into one. Nevertheless, the truth must be told. I was not born in a workhouse, neither am I a twin, for my brother John was considerably my senior; nor was I christened "Lord". How I got that latter title is quite another guitar, which must be tinkled in its proper place. But I was certainly born in Newbury, the facts being on this wise.

When my father came to the Berkshire town he took a house from a man named Halton. This house is still standing, almost opposite the gates of the gasworks, leading out of the Market Place. Here on December 23rd, 1827, I first saw the light, being the sixth child of my parents, who eventually had ten in all, I being the youngest boy.

At the time I was born my father, having built another caravan, fixed up a peep-show, and manufactured an exceedingly primitive roundabout, used to travel the fairs five months in the year as a showman. The other seven months he devoted to trading between London and Newbury, bringing to the latter town fruit, fish, and various other articles, which he sold from a stall erected every Thursday in the Market Place. The statue of the late Queen Victoria, which in these latter years it has been my privilege to present to my native town, stands upon the very spot my father's stall used to occupy.

# CHAPTER III

## THE BATTLE OF OXFORD ROAD

AS I have said, my father had manufactured a very primitive kind of roundabout, which he carried with him as an adjunct to his peep-show. The horses were enlarged examples of the rough penny toys that please the little ones even now. Their legs were simply stiff round sticks. Their bodies were lumps of deal rounded on one side. Their heads were roughly cut from half-inch deal boards, and inserted in a groove in the bodies, while the tails and manes were made of strips of rabbit-skin. They were gaudy animals, however, their coats of paint being white, plentifully dotted with red and blue spots. Motive power was obtained from the boys at the fairs, who, having no half-pennies of their own, were always ready to push round their luckier companions for the reward of a ride later on. My first vivid recollection of going out with this machine and with the peep-show and caravan dates from when I was five years old. It is fixed in my memory because of the great fight between the showmen on the Oxford road – a fight, by the way, that nearly cost the lives of my brother William and myself.

The first fair of the year was always the Mayday gathering at Reading, and showmen of all descriptions moved out of their winter quarters to attend it. We, of course, went from Newbury, with everything spick and span, to attract the public who thronged the place, the fair extending at that time right away down to the river-side, through the whole of the Forbury. This particular year, namely 1833, the collection of larger shows was unusually great, all the giants of the profession at that day – Wombwell, Nelson Lee, Hilton, Randall, Taylor, and the rest – being there in full strength. We had pitched on a very good position, and did excellent business, little expecting what was to follow.

Directly Reading fair was over – it only lasted for one day – all the showmen used to pack up as hurriedly as possible, and, taking little or no rest, make as rapidly as possible to Henley for the fair there on May 3rd. At this time Wombwell's and Hilton's were the two great menageries, and engaged in deadly rivalry. Wombwell's No. 1

collection – for he had two smaller ones – was at Reading fair, and rejoiced in the possession of a giraffe, a rhinoceros, and two elephants, as well as the usual lions, tigers, and smaller carnivora. Against these extra attractions, Hilton's, a very good ordinary collection, could only set an enormous elephant, weighing three tons; and jealously grew apace.

Wombwell's got away from Reading first, closely followed by Hilton's, and behind the latter came a motley string of shows. There was Nelson Lee, with his original Richardson's Booth; Fred Randall, "The Giant"; Sam Taylor, from Ilkeston; another very tall man showing as a giant; "Fat Tom," an enormous personage, exhibited as "the heaviest man on earth"; "Skinny Jack," the North American "Living Skeleton," with the big Holden booth; "Bob," the armless man, who painted pictures with his feet; and many others, including our humble selves – each show having a little army of assistants and hangers-on.

About two miles from Reading, on the Oxford road, the trouble began. Hilton's drivers tried to pass Wombwell's, and at Henley it was first come first served, and those on the ground first secured the best pitches. Wombwell's men drew across the road in such a way as to prevent the passage of their rivals. The wrangle stopped all the shows behind the menageries, as nothing could pass the great animal wagons.

All at once one of Hilton's men knocked one of Wombwell's drivers off his seat with a tent-pole. In a minute all was confusion; grooms, drivers, and carriage attendants of the two menageries left their posts and, catching up any weapons they could lay their hands on – crowbars, tent-poles, whips, etc. – attacked each other with desperate ferocity.

Then the rest of the showmen took sides, for in the profession Hilton's and Wombwell's each had their supporters, and in less than a quarter of an hour a battle was being waged on the Oxford road, at three in the morning, such as had not been seen since the time of the Civil Wars. Even the freaks took part. The fat man made for the living skeleton with a door-hook; the living skeleton battered at the fat man with a peg mallet. Windows and doors of caravans were smashed, and men were lying about bleeding and senseless from wounds.

While the melee was at its height there came a terrible diversion. The horses drawing Wombwell's elephants, left unattended, had taken fright at the noise made by the fighting, swearing men, and the wild beasts who, aroused by the combat, added their howling to the din. Rushing madly away, the powerful team had got too close to one of the deep ditches – dykes we called them then – that bordered the road, the wheels of the great van left the level, and, with a crash, the vehicle turned over.

In two minutes the elephants, mad with fright, had smashed the sides of the wagon to splinters, and made their way out, rushing hither and thither, and turning over everything in their path.

Meanwhile I and my brother William, who was two years older than myself, were standing, two little trembling figures, in our night-gowns at the window of our caravan, which lay some hundred yards behind the string of larger shows, trying to make out what was the matter. We were quite alone, for mother had been left in Reading to come on next day, and father, when the row began on the road, had gone to see what it was all about.

All at once something frightened our horse, and he started to run away, with the result that in another minute we suffered the same fate as Wombwell's elephants, and were turned over into the ditch with a crash that set us screaming at the top of our voices with fright. It was just as well that we did scream, for, in falling over, the fire in our caravan was thrown out and set fire to the vehicle. We should inevitably have been burnt to death had not our voices attracted the attention of some the fight, and who, getting water from the ditch, poured it through the broken window, put out the flames, and rescued us, bruised, frightened, and wet from our predicament.

When the fight was over several men badly hurt were conveyed back to Reading to the hospital, some of them only to come out again as cripples for life. Others were taken on to Henley to be attended by local doctors, and it was looked upon as little short of a miracle that no lives were lost.

Father, hearing of our accident, soon got back to us, and our wagon, which was not much damaged beyond the breaking of the windows and the scorching of the inside, was got upon the road, and we proceeded on our way.

Wombwell's great elephant van was left all smashed up where it had fallen, and the recaptured elephants were walked into the town. We had a good day after all for business, though it was the sorriest lot of battered performers and damaged caravans that Henley fair had ever witnessed.

I have always felt very thankful for the escape of my brother and myself from death, and though I have had several "close calls" since then, as I shall relate in their proper place, nothing has ever more impressed itself on my mind than the scene I witnessed and the danger I escaped from on that memorable May morning on the Oxford road.

# CHAPTER IV

## MAKING THE MOST OF A TRAGEDY

BESIDES the great fight on the Oxford road, many other things went to make the year 1833 a memorable one for me. It was a year of episodes that, despite my tender age, fixed themselves indelibly upon my memory. My father was continually saying to us, "Keep your eyes and ears open. You never know but what something heard or seen may prove of value to you." I have followed his advice all my life, and am thankful that I was able to profit by it from my earliest years.

Though such a little fellow I was always trying to help my parents, and amongst other things soon learned the "patter" in connection with the pictures in our peep-show. The latter, by the way, was an enormous improvement on the one wherewith my father started life on the road. To my childish mind it was indeed "the greatest show on earth," and some of the proudest hours of my existence came in this year when I was allowed in my shrill treble to call the attention of the fair-going crowds to its glories.

It had twenty-six glasses, so that twenty-six persons could see the views at the same time, the pictures being pulled up and down by strings. At night it was illuminated by a row of tallow candles set between the pictures and the observer, and requiring very regular snuffing. No doubt the candles, placed as they were, detracted from the effect of the pictures, but people in those days were not so particular as they are now, and as long as they had plenty of colour in the backgrounds were perfectly satisfied.

Anyhow, I thought it perfection, and was a proud mite as, with a clean pinafore and well-greased boots, I stood outside and asked the folks to "Walk up! Walk up!" Tragedies were always strong points with peep-shows, and one of our attractions at that time was a series of scenes representing the "Murder in the Red Barn".

"Walk up!" I would pipe, "walk up and see the only correct views of the terrible murder of Maria Martin. They are historically accurate and true to life, depicting the death of Maria at the hands of the villain Corder in the famous Red Barn. You will see how the

## CONFESSION AND EXECUTION OF

# WILLIAM CORDER,

### THE MURDERER OF MARIA MARTEN.

Since the tragical affair between Thurtell and Weare, no event has occurred connected with the criminal annals of our country which has excited so much interest as the trial of Corder, who was justly convicted of the murder of Maria Marten on Friday last.

### THE CONFESSION.

"Bury Gaol, August 10th, 1828.—Condemned cell.
"Sunday evening, half-past Eleven.

"I acknowledge being guilty of the death of poor Maria Marten, by shooting her with a pistol. The particulars are as follows :—When we left her father's house, we began quarrelling about the burial of the child: she apprehended the place wherein it was deposited would be found out. The quarrel continued about three quarters of an hour upon this sad and about other subjects. A scuffle ensued, and during the scuffle, and at the time I think that she had hold of me, I took the pistol from the side pocket of my velveteen jacket and fired. She fell, and died in an instant. I never saw her even struggle. I was overwhelmed with agitation and dismay :—the body fell near the front doors on the floor of the barn  A vast quantity of blood issued from the wound, and ran on to the floor and through the crevices. Having determined to bury the body in the barn (about two hours after she was dead. I went and borrowed a spade of Mrs Stow, but before I went there I dragged the body from the barn into the chaff-house, and locked the barn. I returned again to the barn, and began to dig a hole, but the spade being a bad one, and the earth firm and hard, I was obliged to go home for a pickaxe and a better spade, with which I dug the hole, and then buried the body. I think I dragged the body by the handkerchief that was tied round her neck. It was dark when I finished covering up the body. I went the next day, and washed the blood from off the barn-floor. I declare to Almighty God I had no sharp instrument about me, and no other wound but the one made by the pistol was inflicted by me. I have been guilty of great idleness, and at times led a dissolute life, but I hope through the mercy of God to be forgiven. WILLIAM CORDER."

Witness to the signing by the said William Corder,
JOHN ORRIDGE.

Condemned cell, Eleven o'clock, Monday morning, August 11th, 1828.

The above confession was read over carefully to the prisoner in our presence, who stated most solemnly it was true, and that he had nothing to add to or retract from it.—W. STOCKING, chaplain ; TIMOTHY R. HOLMES, Under-Shertff.

### THE EXECUTION.

At ten minutes before twelve o'clock the prisoner was brought from his cell and pinioned by the hangman, who was brought from London for the purpose. He appeared resigned, but was so weak as to be unable to stand without support; when his cravat was removed he groaned heavily, and appeared to be labouring under great mental agony. When his wrists and arms were made fast, he was led round twards the scaffold, and as he passed the different yards in which the prisoners were confined, he shook hands with them, and speaking to two of them by name, he said, "Good bye, God bless you." They appeared considerably affected by the wretched appearance which he made, and "God bless you !" "May God receive your soul !" were frequently uttered as he passed along. The chaplain walked before the prisoner, reading the usual Burial Service, and the Governor and Officers walking immediately after him. The prisoner was supported to the steps which led to the scaffold ; he looked somewhat wildly around, and a constable was obliged to support him while the hangman was adjusting the fatal cord. There was a barrier to keep off the crowd, amounting to upwards of 7,000 persons, who at this time had stationed themselves in the adjoining fields, on the hedges, the tops of houses, and at every point from which a view of the execution could be best obtained. The prisoner, a few moments before the drop fell, groaned heavily, and would have fallen, had not a second constable caught hold of him. Everything having been made ready, the signal was given, the fatal drop fell, and the unfortunate man was launched into eternity. Just before he was turned off, he said in a feeble tone, "I am justly sentenced, and may God forgive me."

## The Murder of Maria Marten.

### BY W. CORDER.

COME all you thoughtless young men, a warning take by
  me,
And think upon my unhappy fate to be hanged upon a tree ;
My name is William Corder, to you I do declare,
I courted Maria Marten, most beautiful and fair.

I promised I would marry her upon a certain day,
Instead of that, I was resolved to take her life away.
I went into her father's house the 18th day of May,
Saying, my dear Maria, we will fix the wedding day.

If you will meet me at the Red-barn, as sure as I have life,
I will take you to Ipswich town, and there make you my wife ;
I then went home and fetched my gun, my pickaxe and my spade,
I went into the Red-barn, and there I dug her grave.

With heart so light, she thought no harm, to meet him she did go
He murdered her all in the barn, and laid her body low ;
After the horrible deed was done, she lay weltering in her gore,
Her bleeding mangled body he buried beneath the Red-barn floor.

Now all things being silent, her spirit could not rest,
She appeared unto her mother, who suckled her at her breast ;
For many a long month or more, her mind being sore oppress'd,
Neither night or day she could not take any rest.

Her mother's mind being so disturbed, she dreamt three nights
  o'er,
Her daughter she lay murdered beneath the Red-barn floor ;
She sent the father to the barn, when he the ground did thrust,
And there he found his daughter mingling with the dust.

My trial is hard, I could not stand, most woeful was the sight,
When her jaw-bone was brought to prove, which pierced my
  heart quite ;
Her aged father standing by, likewise his loving wife,
And in her grief her hair she tore, she scarcely could keep life.

Adieu, adieu, my loving friends, my glass is almost run,
On Monday next will be my last, when I am to be hang'd ;
So you, young men, who do pass by, with pity look on me,
For murdering Maria Marten, I was haug'd upon the tree.

Printed by J. Catnach, 2 and 3, Monmouth Court.—Cards, &c., Printed Cheap.

ghost of Maria appeared to her mother on three successive nights at the bedside, leading to the discovery of the body and the arrest of Corder at Eveley Grove House, Brentford, seven miles from London."

When we had our row of spectators getting their pennyworths from the peep-holes I would describe the various pictures as they were pulled up into view. The arrest of Corder was always given special prominence, as follows: "The arrest of the murderer Corder as he was at breakfast with the two Miss Singletons. Lee, the officer, is seen entering the door and telling Corder of the serious charge against him. Observe the horrified faces of the ladies, and note, also, so true to life are these pictures, that even the saucepan is shown upon the fire and the minute-glass upon the table timing the boiling of the eggs!"

After hours of this sort of thing, and when the fair had closed, there came a bit of supper in the living-wagon, and then I would kneel down at my dear mother's knee to say my prayers, for these she would never allow us to forget. These over, I would tumble into bed, a tired but happy boy, to sleep soundly as the show moved on through the early morning to some other stopping-place, my father snatching a few hours' rest as best he could.

The last big fair of the year was the Statute at Wantage, in Berkshire, held on October 18th, and here another incident occurred, which not only filled my childish mind with horror, but also greatly impressed upon me my father's readiness and resource.

We got into the town the day before the fair, and late in the afternoon, having secured his pitch, my father went to have a glass of ale at the "Red Lion." While he was there several labourers entered the inn, and amongst them a man who had been engaged in field-work and carried a "fagging-hook," something like that used for reaping. The fellow called for a pint of ale, and not being very quickly served, got into a dispute with the landlady, who apparently had had some trouble with him on previous occasions, and who soundly rated him.

When at last the ale was brought, the labourer, instead of putting the coppers to pay for it on the table, dropped them on the floor. The landlady, with a few more angry words, stooped to pick them up. As she did so, without a word of warning, the wretch struck her a terrible blow across the neck with his fagging-hook, nearly severing her head from her body. In an instant all was confusion. A rush was made upon the cowardly murderer, who struck out right and left, but was eventually overpowered and taken to the lock-up, while the poor woman's body was put into an empty room to await an inquest.

I well remember the excitement in the town and amongst the show-folk caused by the terrible tragedy, and how we children bothered mother with questions as to what it was all about.

We were silent as mice, and our eyes were round with horror as father told the tale in our caravan that night. I can almost hear him now as he denounced the murderer, and told us never to let our passions lead us into crime. "Keep your temper, my boys, keep your temper," he said. "Never lift a hand to a human being except in self-defence, and never seek a quarrel." Those words have been with me all my life. They have meant much to me, and their remembrance has more than once, though often grievously provoked, kept me from entering into disputes which I should afterwards have deeply regretted.

The next day all the talk of the fair was the tragedy at the "Red Lion," and my father, much as it had horrified him, saw a showman's opportunity in it. He had some pictures by him that with a little artful alteration might be made to resemble somewhat the scene of the murder. The figure of a woman, I remember, was cut out of another picture, and with the head removed was pasted in as if prone on the floor of the taproom, the latter picture, by the way, having formerly done duty in "The Murder at the Roadside Inn"; the head of the woman was then fixed as if lying some little distance from the body; a ferocious-looking figure with a sickle was introduced, and with a plentiful supply of carmine for gore the trick was done.

It was really a most effective "fake," and we did splendidly with it, crowds flocking to our show to see "the authentic representation of the terrible murder at the 'Red Lion,' as described by an eyewitness of the dreadful deed." The "patter" concerning this and similar occurrences, I may here remark has undoubtedly done much to preserve them in my memory, and to render more vivid the recollections of these very early days.

# CHAPTER V

## THE SCOURGE, AND SOME STRANGE REMEDIES

AS I have said, we did splendidly with our hastily improvised tragedy scene, the only drawback being that at the finish of the fair we found we had with good money taken also a considerable amount that was bad, despite a sharp look-out for the latter kept by my father and mother. Such a look-out was especially necessary at Wantage, which had at that period, and, indeed, for some years afterwards, a most unenviable reputation for the manufacture of base coin. Certain local families who went to markets and fairs in the district with ginger-bread stalls were suspected, and, indeed, amongst the show-folk were known to be engaged in dealing in the spurious currency. So poor, however, were the police arrangements that the "smashers" were very rarely caught, though on one occasion, I believe, a little before my time, no fewer than seven Wantage coiners were sentenced to death at Reading Assizes. What bad coin my father took he religiously broke up. He had the greatest detestation of coiners, as being "heartless robbers of the poor", and he always impressed it on us children that it was our duty to destroy any bad coin that came into our possession, lest it should become the cause of misery to others possibly worse off than ourselves. Since then in my business I have taken much bad money, but my dear old dad's advice was never forgotten, and after the spurious stuff reached me I always took good care that nobody else suffered by it.

From Wantage fair we made our way direct to Newbury to commence, as we hoped, our winter business of the fish and vegetable trade. But though we had done well on the road with our show our hearts were far from light. There was a blight upon the land. With the autumn had come rumours of wildly spreading disease that was devastating the towns and the countryside in the North, and was rapidly making its presence felt in the Midlands.

There was an atmosphere of uneasiness that affected even us children. We could see that father and mother were unusually disturbed. Now and then we caught snatches of conversations, sometimes between mother and father, sometimes between our parents and others on the road. From these conversations, always hushed when we little ones drew near, we gathered that "it", whatever that dreadful "it" might be, was "spreading terribly," that there had been awful scenes in "such and such a place," that in some places "the dead-carts were busy night and day."

At night in the caravan, when our prayer-time came, mother, and very often father with her, would pray that we might be kept from "the scourge," that the evil might be allowed to pass us by, and we little ones listened and wondered, and trembled in our beds with the fear of the unknown.

It was not till we reached Newbury that we children heard the name of the dreadful thing, the fear of which was so worrying our parents. Then we heard that it was the small-pox – small-pox in its most virulent form – that was ravaging England in a way that for violence had not been known since an outbreak twenty years before.

People in these days cannot imagine what the scourge was like; what a thrill of fear and horror its name produced. Isolated cases were in those days always to be found. In some places, notably in seaport towns, the slums of London, and other large cities, it lurked regularly, and people were, in a sense, accustomed to its presence. But now and again, as in the autumn of this year – 1833 – it burst forth into a tremendous pestilence that stalked the length and breadth of the land.

I shall never forget that time of horror, the dreadful impression it had upon my mind as a child; nor shall I ever cease to thank God for giving me for a parent a man so wise in his humble way, so strong and self-reliant, as my father proved to be in battling with this great sickness.

On the evening of the day after our return to Newbury father came in and told mother that the scourge was in the town and was spreading rapidly. That night there were some very earnest prayers offered for our safety in our little dwelling, and father told us that we must not give way to fear; everything was in the hands of God, who did all things for the best.

But we were not to escape. The next night the dreadful thing was with us. My little sister, a year younger than myself, who had been ailing some days, was stricken down. Poor little girl, she had it very badly, and though she recovered, was pitted in a dreadful way.

What a time of trouble that was! My mother, wan and pale, watched night and day with her sick child, who was, of course, rigorously shut away from the rest of us. Outside all was as mournful as it was indoors. The church bell was continually tolling for the dead, and hurried funerals were everywhere being conducted. Business was stopped, and nobody thrived except the undertakers.

Father, however, never lost heart, but battled with the trouble in his own fashion. There was no vaccination then, but he had heard and seen something of the benefits of inoculation as a check to the disease, and was bold enough to carry out the process.

When the pustules on my sister were fully developed, he got us other children together and operated on us. His instrument was a long darning needle. This he passed right through the upper part of the muscle of each one's right arm. Then into the tiny wound on each side he rubbed a little of the serum taken from the pustules of the sufferer. I cannot think of the operation even now without a shudder, but the results were all that could be wished.

Each of us rapidly developed the disease, but in the mildest possible form. I know that I myself was only ill a few days, and that very slightly, and that only a few spots appeared on my skin. Some of the others were worse than I was, but none of us was really very bad.

The worse part of the business was the nauseous medicine he made us take while the sickness was upon us. He compounded it himself, nor did I nor any of the others know what its composition was. Whence he got this extraordinary recipe I do not know, but he firmly believed in its efficacy. Anyhow, we all got better, and none of us took the small-pox afterwards, though I am inclined to believe, having witnessed the wonderful results of vaccination in later days, that it was the inoculation rather than the draught, unpleasant to think of, let alone to swallow, that saved us from the horrors we saw around us.

News of my father's treatment soon spread, and seeing its good results, dozens, nay hundreds, of people came to be inoculated themselves, and to have their children operated on, and to carry off doses of the famous secret medicine. Many of these people occupied exceedingly high positions. Some of them were even sent to my father by doctors who knew him, and who were aware that we were an exceedingly healthy family.

In after years, remembering what inoculation had saved us from, I did all I could to encourage the practice of vaccination. On the Continent small-pox in the old days was very rampant, and on several of my early tours I was myself vaccinated, and urged my example on my company, with the result that I never lost but one or two from smallpox in the whole course of my career, and in each case the victims were unvaccinated persons. It is certainly the fact that when I was a young man two out of every six persons you met were pitted with small-pox. Now a pitted person is a rarity, and so is the disease, owing, I firmly believe, to the general practice of vaccination. That, however, is a digression, but I could not refrain from making it, and I sincerely trust that England will never again undergo such an awful visitation as that which so impressed and terrified me when I was a little child.

# CHAPTER VI

## A GHASTLY ADVENTURE

WHEN the rage of the small-pox had abated and the family were all quite well again we commenced our usual winter business of carrying fish, fruit, and vegetables from London and Southampton to Newbury and the villages. We had not long started it when a ghastly adventure befell me and my father – an adventure which for a long time haunted me in my sleep and gave me hideous dreams.

We were returning from London with fish and other things when we stopped at a roadside inn, the "Bell and Bottle," which still exists, some few miles above Reading, in order to rest and feed the horses. In those days such houses were open day and night for the accommodation of travellers on the road. Father was, of course, well known, and when he went into the bar-parlour for some refreshment was asked by some friends to join in a game of cards. As he had a least an hour to stop he agreed, and sat down to enjoy himself.

I was in and out of the house several times, first watching the card-players, then going to see that the wagon and horses were all right, and so on. I had just come in from one of my visits to the wagon, which, by the way, was a long, four-wheeled vehicle, when somebody, coming to the bar-parlour door, said father was wanted. "Who is it?" asked father, not wishing to be disturbed at his game; "let him come here."

Next minute a stranger appeared, a rather tall, respectable-looking man I recollect, dressed in the usual smock-frock of the countryside. "Oh," said the new-comer, "Mr. Sanger, I and my two mates are in a bit of a difficulty. We've got to get to Reading with our parcel of duds and things for a little job, and can find no conveyance. Will you give us a lift that far?"

"Certainly," said my father, in his kindly, easygoing way. "Put your duds on the back rail of the wagon, we've nothing there to carry, and you can come along. I shall be ready to start," he added, "in a quarter of an hour."

This was a hint for me, so I went out and saw the stranger and his mates lift their parcel, a pretty heavy sack full of goods it seemed, on to the back of our wagon. Then they all got on to the front of the vehicle to ride. Father hadn't bargained for their riding, but as the horses were well rested, and Reading was not many miles away, he said nothing when he came out of the "Bell and Bottle," and taking his place at the horses' heads; started them once more on the road.

It was a cold, frosty morning early in January. The roads were hard and good, and the old moon was flooding the country with her silver light, making everything almost as bright as day. Never have I seen bright moonlight since without that morning journey coming to my recollection, so strongly do some events fix themselves on the mind.

My father and I walked on by the horses while our passengers on the front of the wagon laughed and talked, and one of them started singing a coarse song, but stopped when my father objected. Then for some reason I fell a bit behind the wagon, and as I did so I noticed the parcel the men had put on the back showing out in the strong moonlight. It was a bulky, long, shapeless sort of bundle contained in a big sack, and it wobbled in a fashion that made it seem, to my boyish eyes, as though it had something alive in it. This roused my curiosity, though at the same time it gave me a creepy kind of feeling.

However, I did not look closer, but got back to the horses' heads and plodded along with father, thinking, however, all the time of the curious wobbling bundle at our back. Presently, when we had gone, perhaps, another mile, father stopped at the roadside, and the wagon passed him as it had done in my case. He was some few minutes before he rejoined me, and when I looked at his face I was frightened, it was so stern and set. Something had evidently upset him, but he said nothing, and we plodded on as before.

After travelling for some half a mile farther I let the wagon again pass me, and fell behind it, my eyes once more fixed on the mysterious parcel at the back. This time my curiosity overcame me. I swung myself up to the wagon rail and took a close look at the bundle. I could see the neck of the sack was unloosed, as though somebody had recently untied it, and pulling the sack aside I peeped in.

Oh! my God, the horror of that moment! I hung to the rail paralysed with fear. The moonlight shone clearly through the loosened sack, and I saw a naked human arm and the pallid wax-like face of a dead woman!

Why I did not scream out I cannot tell from that day to this. But I did not. I simply dropped off the back of the wagon shaking with fear, my knees giving way under me so that I could not walk. Indeed, when I recovered myself, the wagon was some distance ahead, and I had to run to catch it.

When I got to my father's side he evidently saw by my white face and shaking form that I had discovered what we were carrying, for he caught hold of my shoulder, and stooping down said in a stern whisper, "Don't speak, Georgie, not a word! Keep on by the side of the horses!"

I obeyed him, and walked on as if in a dream, with the face of the dead woman before my eyes seeming to bob at me with every movement of the animals. I walked mechanically, seeing nothing except that awful face, nor did I rouse out of my stupor until we were within two miles of Reading.

Here we came up with another wagon whose team had stopped to rest. Our strange passengers had drowsed off, and seemingly did not notice our movements. I kept on by the horses while my father stopped to speak to the resting wagoner. Another minute and the latter's boy passed me in the moonlight racing as if for his life towards the town, and I heard the jangle of the bells on the horses' heads as with a hoarse "Gee!" the wagoner behind us started his team to follow ours.

So we moved on for perhaps another mile when suddenly I heard the hum of voices. My father stopped his horses, and in a few minutes our wagon was surrounded by a crowd of people armed with pitchforks, cudgels, and other rustic weapons. Our passengers, roused from their slumbers, were speedily pulled off the wagon, and when my father had explained what had occurred and some of the folk had seen the dreadful thing we carried, the three men, greeted as "Murderers!" with their hands tied with wagon cords, and evidently overwhelmed with fear, were hustled with many curses and smart blows from cudgels towards Reading.

Near the town we were met by a party of constables, who took charge of the prisoners. It was well for the latter that they did so, for the men would undoubtedly have been beaten to death when it was made known that the case was not one of murder, but something even more abhorrent to the public mind at that time – namely, body-snatching.

# CHAPTER VII
## THE BODY-SNATCHERS

THE three men turned out to be well-known resurrectionists, who found a market for their horrible wares in the medical school at Oxford. The poor woman had been buried on the morning of the day prior to our call at the "Bell and Bottle" in a little village churchyard not far from the inn, and the grave had been rifled the same night.

They had carried the body to an outhouse of the inn, and failing to get a cart they expected, had adopted the means I have related to get it carried to Reading. Their intention was to have taken it off about half a mile from the town, where they had confederates who could provide a light cart, and when that arrived the body would have been packed in and driven to Oxford without anybody being the wiser.

All this, of course, I learned much later from my father. The latter, going behind the wagon, as I have related, noticed, as I did, the curious shape of the bundle in the moonlight, and undoing the mouth of the sack, made the discovery which so horrified me afterwards. He at once made up his mind what to do, and the lucky drowsiness of the body-snatchers helped his purpose and enabled their capture.

They received, I believe, long terms of imprisonment, and my father, I know, was greatly commended for his action, which was the talk of the road for many a long day afterwards. As for myself, I was for a time very sick and ill, and months later would start from my sleep, shrieking that I saw a dead woman's face near mine.

Imagine it, you who have any nerves at all, what effect such an adventure had upon a boy of my tender age. True, I was bold beyond my years through early contact with the world, but I was, none the less, highly impressionable and nervous. It was my first and only personal experience of the terrible business of body-snatching that was then regularly carried on. I thank God that I never saw anything of it afterwards, though I heard much about it and went with others who had business on the roads at night in dread of the "burkers," who were supposed to secure victims for the dissecting table by choking them with pitch-plaisters.

Those dreadful days, thanks to the passing of the Anatomy Act, have long been at an end, and are now only a memory, horribly vivid in my case, to old men like myself; while those of the present generation can scarcely conceive them. But they formed part and parcel of my first and worst experiences of that life on the road the story of which I am now endeavouring to set forth.

# CHAPTER VIII

## HOW THE CHARTISTS SPOILED NEWPORT FAIR

WINTER over, we prepared once more for our business on the road as showmen, and May-day, 1839, found us, as usual, at the opening fair of the season, at Reading, with our peep-show and roundabout. This year father resolved to go farther afield, and we made our way from one fair to another, till we eventually found ourselves in South Wales.

Here, again, new ground was to give us new adventures to introduce us to scenes that were to be fixed indelibly upon my memory.

We arrived at Newport, in Monmouthshire, in time for the fair annually held on Whit-Thursday, hoping for good business, as the gathering was always a large one, well attended by the miners, who were reputed to be free with their money. Very little of it, however, was to come to us, or, indeed, to any of the showmen on this occasion, excitement of quite another kind being provided for the town, much to our dismay.

After we had reached Newport, the night before the fair, and got our pitch, father, as usual, went out to get his glass of ale with the other folk, and to learn what was doing. He came back, looking terribly worried and upset, and mother said, "James, I can see something is wrong. What is it?"

"Everything! Everything, my dear!" was his reply. Then, as we children listened open-mouthed, he told her that the Chartists had picked the fair day for a great demonstration. From thirty to forty thousand miners, he had been told, were coming into the town next morning, and, it was feared, would wreck and pillage the place. In any case, it was certain that the fair would be spoiled, and that all chances of our making a little money out of it were at an end. It was a dreadful situation for us, and I remember, as if it were only yesterday, how mother burst into tears, and we little ones cried with her in sympathy.

"What will become of us, James? What will become of us?" said poor mother.

"We must make the best of it," said father, "and trust Providence to pull us through. Now, you children, say your prayers and get to bed, for we must be moving very early to get out of this."

Prayers were said – earnest prayers, too, I can assure you – asking for help and safety for the poor showman and his family, and then we all turned in, though we did not sleep much, so full were we of fear of what the morrow might bring to us.

Soon after dawn father roused us all to assist in packing up our show, which was pitched in the old cattle market, and very soon our booth, from which we had hoped so much, was down, and our effects were being stowed in the wagon. All round us showmen were similarly engaged in preparing for flight, so great was the dread inspired by the miners, whose roughness  and brutality were at that time proverbial. When all was ready, off we started to get out of the town, which we children veritably believed was about to be destroyed. Indeed, nobody foresaw what a farcical finish this "terrible attack" of the Chartists on Newport would result in. So we trembled as we went helter-skelter up the road, our fears being mightily increased by what we saw when we got near the Westgate Hotel, the old pillars of which, by the way, still bear witness of what occurred on that momentous Whitsuntide fair day.

Just as we reached the hotel, we saw perhaps a hundred men coming down the long hill into the town. As they came into view gangs of roughs began to pour through the alley-ways from the dockside to join the Chartist procession, shouting and swearing in a way that made us quake with fear.

Father hurried on our wagon as fast as he could, but when we got about a mile from the town we saw a tremendous crowd of people coming down the road, and there was nothing for it but to pull up close to the roadside to let them pass, and to pray that they might be peaceable in their passage.

They were the Chartist colliers, whose coming we had so dreaded, and I doubt if it is possible for any of you who read this to conceive our feelings as they drew near. If they attacked our wagon and broke it up it meant utter hopeless ruin to us; moreover, there was the awful fear of personal outrage and even murder at their hands. So we sat and waited, and trembled.

On they came, many of them half drunk, yelling, swearing, and waving great cudgels, a terrifying mass of men. It was estimated afterwards that they numbered about thirty thousand, and I should think that for quite two hours they were tramping by our caravan.

Perhaps we were too insignificant for their attention. Anyhow, beyond flinging an occasional volley of oaths at us, we were not interfered with. But it was not until the main body had passed that we drew our breaths freely, and father put down the loaded blunderbuss that, with grim determination to protect his family and property at all costs, he had taken up when the crowd first came into view.

Some little while after the colliers had gone by we heard the sound of firing in the direction of the town. Father got out an old spy-glass he possessed, to see if he could view anything of what was going on. Presently he said, "Into the wagon, all of you! Shut up all the windows and the door. Here they come back again!"

They did come. At a much faster pace than they had gone down the hill they raced back again and very soon were passing our wagon in thousands. This time they were in such a hurry that they did not even stop to swear at us. From what was now and again muttered by them, mother said it was evident that the soldiers were after them, and they were afraid of being shot. But we saw no soldiers, only the hurrying crowd, and when that had passed the road lay quiet and peaceful, the only objects on it being the caravans, dotted here and there by the hedge-side, of show-folk, who, like ourselves, had fled the town, and had drawn up to let the mob go by.

We learned later that the soldiers, who had so frightened and awed the desperate crowd from whom such violence was expected, were only twenty-four in number. This little army was stationed in the Westgate Hotel, and possessed exactly three rounds of ball cartridge.

When the invading Chartists reached the great space in front of the famous old coaching-house they began their threatened campaign of destruction by breaking the windows with stones, having filled their pockets with the latter as they came down the roads. No response being made to their attack, they grew bolder, and presently a number of the colliers made a rush for the hotel gates, with the intention of battering them down, so that they could loot the cellars of the liquor they contained.

Then they got a check. As the first of the crowd reached the big doors the soldiers, who were posted at windows in the wings commanding the entrance, opened fire. Crash! went twenty-four muskets, and down fell two of the leaders of the crowd. The mob was staggered, and before the rioters could recover another volley was poured into them, and more men fell.

That was quite sufficient for the gallant invaders; and, stricken with panic, they turned and fled out of the town, as I have described, their movements being hastened by a rumour, quite an unfounded one, that the cavalry were coming. As a matter of fact, there were no soldiers, save the twenty-four posted at the Westgate Hotel, within ten miles of the town; and these twenty-four, as I have said, had only three rounds of ball cartridge. Had the mob been aware of these facts the result might have been very different. But they did not know it. So twenty-four men drove away twenty-four thousand. Newport remained unpillaged, and the great Chartist demonstration fizzled out.

All the same, it made an excellent subject for my father's peep-show. We very soon had a fancy picture of "The riots at Newport, with an exact delineation," as our patter had it, "of the desperate attack on the Westgate Hotel, the firing on the crowd by the soldiers, and the flight of the mob." I pattered this so often afterwards at the various small fairs and country feasts we visited that the occurrence remains one of my most vivid memories.

In addition to the Newport riots we later added the trial of Frost, Williams, and Jones, the Chartist leaders, to our peep-show. They were sentenced for treason-felony to the old punishment of hanging, drawing, and quartering, but the sentence was, of course, never carried out, and they escaped with various terms of imprisonment.

Father tried to explain to us what the Chartists sought to obtain and what the Charter was from which they took their name. At the time, however, I knew little about it, though I could patter volubly enough about the riots and the trial. But I have since lived to see nearly everything granted in the way of liberty that the Chartists then asked for, with none of the evil results that people in the old days so freely prophesied would follow.

# CHAPTER IX

## THE RAID ON LANSDOWN FAIR

AFTER the fiasco at Newport we attended various small fairs and village wakes, and did very well. I was growing fast and was very tall and strong for my age, and had begun to learn to turn somersaults and to do balancing and other little tricks that were to serve me well in my later career as a showman. Father would never allow any of us to be idle, and all who were big enough had to help with the show in some way.

"Those who won't work shan't eat," he used to say, and I have often since blessed his memory for the training of those early days. He was never harsh or unkind, only firm with us. "Learn to work as children," he used to say, "and you will never be afraid of work when you grow up." I can bear witness to the great truth of utterance, for in my life I have had to do all kinds of toil, and could always do it cheerfully, thanks to the wisdom of my father, and the patient, self-sacrificing kindness of my dear mother, when I was a child.

Our caravan, twelve feet long, just over seven feet wide, and about seven feet high, sheltered, despite hardships, a very happy family, as we travelled from place to place. My father, though but a showman, a very despised profession in those days, knew how to make men and women of us, and with mother taught us to be honest and helpful towards our fellows. Nor was education forgotten. Though I never had but one day's proper schooling, and then was taken away because of a master's harshness, no opportunity was neglected by my parents of giving me lessons in writing and reading. They taught me to value knowledge, and as the years have rolled I have gathered it whenever I could. The results are plain to view, and I ask you, dear readers, to kindly humour the old showman if, as now, he occasionally digresses to honour the memory of those parents whose care and training made him what he is to-day.

From place to place we went with our little show, and at length found ourselves at Lansdown, near Bath, for the big cattle, sheep, and pleasure fair that then used to be held annually on August 10th at the hill village, which is some two miles from the old city.

It was here that I saw an example of the rough justice that the showmen occasionally meted out to their enemies and tormentors, who in those days were legion. Such things could not happen now, for we live in better times, the arm of the law is longer, and life and property have safeguards that in those days were not dreamt of. Men then had to protect themselves and their belongings as best they could, and often to right their own wrongs as I saw the showmen do at Lansdown Fair.

Though it was the resort of all the rank and fashion in the land, who came to seek health from the famous waters, and was the home as now of a multitude of wealthy, stately, and dignified personages, who dwelt beneath the shadow of its ancient cathedral, Bath had at that time a very unenviable reputation regarded its lower classes. I have, by the way, noticed that most cathedral cities – and in Britain I have visited them all – show remarkable contrasts in regard to their populations. At the top you have all that is best in the way of piety and learning, all that is enviable in the way of ease and dignity. At the bottom you will find dirt, degradation, misery, and evil of the most appalling kinds. Why this should be I cannot say, but I have certainly observed it. Anyhow, Bath at this period had in its slums what was considered to be the most brutish and criminal mob in England, and for these people Lansdown Fair was, as they put it, "their night out."

Though it lasted but one day, the fair was always a big one, occupying a great space on a broad hillside. On this booths, shows, and refreshment tents of all descriptions were erected to form an enormous ring, in the centre of which were the droves of sheep, cattle, and horses that formed the staple of the fair to which the country-folk flocked from all the district round.

On this occasion the gathering was a very great one. All the best-known showmen in the country were there, money was plentiful, and throughout the day we did exceedingly well. As dusk came on the regular business people – the farmers, graziers, and others who had been dealing in the horses, cattle, farm produce, and such-like – left the fair to the pleasure-seekers. The drinking booths, gingerbread stalls, and shows began to twinkle with lights. Twinkle is the only word that fits the illumination of fairs in those days.

Recollect it was before the time of the naphtha lamps. We had only candles, the commonest of dips and rushlights, for inside work, and these kept numbers of people busy the night long doing nothing else but snuffing them. Outside the booths hung flares – horrible, odorous things, consisting of three prongs set in a shallow iron or tin dish. Rags were rolled up and put into these prongs, then round about were packed lumps of rough tallow, that melted and kept the rag-wick supplied with fat after it was lit. These flares were slung up with three chains to the booth poles, and their spluttering, smoky flame was our chief illuminant. Think of it, you who only know the brilliance of gas and electricity, and you may be able to realize something of the disadvantages that night brought to those old-time showmen.

As night advanced the character of the fair crowd gradually changed. It grew rougher and rougher. Fights were frequent. Oaths and screams were mingled with coarse songs from the drinking and dancing booths, which were filled with a motley throng. Business at our peep-show and with our roundabout became slacker and slacker, till at last, about ten o'clock, father gave the word to close up. Even as he did so a terrible row broke out amongst the booths nearest the Bath road, and very soon we got the news that the Bath roughs were out in force, bent on mischief.

How we toiled and hurried to make our belongings as safe as possible! Everything that could be broken or stolen was hastily packed in or under the living-wagon, and made secure with chains and bolts. At last we finished, and then with every light out so as not to attract attention, we sat and listened to the turmoil that was now raging all round us.

The roughs were led by a red-headed virago, a dreadful giantess of a woman, known as "Carroty Kate". She was an awful creature, strong as a navvy, a big brutal animal, caring nothing for magistrates or gaol, and had long been the terror of every respectable person in Bath and its neighbourhood. With the majority of her followers, she hailed from Bull Paunch Alley, the lowest slum in the cathedral city, where no policeman ever dared to penetrate, and innumerable horrors were committed nightly.

Half stripped, with her red hair flying wildly behind her, she incited the gang of ruffians with her to wreck the fair. The drinking booths were the first to suffer. The mob took possession of them, half killed some of the unfortunate owners, and then set to work to drink themselves into a state of frenzy even more acute than before. The scenes that followed are almost indescribable. Not content with drinking all they could, the ruffians turned on the taps, staved in barrels, smashed up bottles, and let the liquor run to waste. Then they started to wreck the booths. Canvas was torn to shreds, platforms were smashed up and made bonfires of, wagons were battered and overturned, show-fronts that had cost some of their poor owners small fortunes were battered to fragments. Everywhere was riot, ruin, and destruction.

# CHAPTER X

## SHOWMEN'S LYNCH LAW

THE few police that were about were utterly helpless, and the show-folk had to protect themselves as best they could, some of them making a very manful fight against overpowering numbers. Assistance, it was said, had been sent for by the authorities, but if that was so it did not arrive until the mischief was complete. We children and poor mother were in a state of fear that can well be imagined. Father had told us to get ready to run away up the hillside and to lie down on the grass if the mob came towards our caravan, so that we might escape in jury. For himself, he had no fear; he put an extra handful of slugs into the old blunderbuss, meaning to have at least one good shot at the wreckers if they touched the bit of property that was his living.

But the ruffians did not touch us. The mischief was confined chiefly to the lower end of the fair, where everything was practically destroyed, and more than one poor traveller brought close to ruin. As dawn broke the riot died down, and the drunken mob, glutted with the wanton destruction of the belongings of poor people who had never done them any harm, began to straggle, shouting, swearing, and singing, back towards Bath.

Then, by ones and twos, the showmen came together, pale with anger, some of them bruised and bleeding from the fray, and all resolved on vengeance. They had marked one or two of the ringleaders of the riot, and meant to give them a taste of showmen's law. The scene is before me now as I saw it when I stood with my brother William, still pale with fear, but full of childish curiosity, on the steps of our caravan, in the dawnlight, and watched some thirty stalwart showmen, my father amongst them, armed with stout cudgels, mount the hastily collected wagon horses, and, bare-backed, ride after the retreating mob.

Presently the riders returned, dragging with them as prisoners about a dozen men and the terrible woman "Carroty Kate", with their hands tied behind them. They who had been the bold leaders of the attack on the booths now shook with fear, as the drink evaporated, and they found themselves in the hands of the men they had so wantonly injured.

All the show-folk, young and old, turned out to see the punishment of the rioters, which was carried out with a precision and thoroughness that deeply impressed me. First of all, the woman was securely fastened to the wheel of a heavy wagon, and was left cursing us as we followed the male prisoners down the hill. At the foot there was a deep, wide pond, and there the punishment commenced.

With long tent ropes the showmen linked the wreckers together by their bound hands. Then a stout rope was thrown across the pond and fastened to the living chain, some twenty stalwart showmen holding the line on the farther bank. On the near side father quickly attached another line to the prisoners, which was similarly manned by showmen. All was now ready, and an old van-dweller stepped out and told our prisoners that as it was no use looking to the law to revenge the injuries they had caused the showmen the latter were going to give them a lesson that should be a lasting one. His address was very brief and very emphatic, and when it was finished he threw up his hand and shouted "Go!"

In a moment the prisoners were dragged into the pond. Right across the showmen pulled them with hearty good will. Then back again they were lugged, spluttering and howling for mercy. No notice was taken of their cries, but backwards and forwards through the muddy water they were pulled until no breath was left in their bodies. One or two, indeed, were so still that some of the showmen cried out in alarm that they were drowned.

"No fear," shouted my father, in tones that I can hear even yet. "That sort doesn't die from drowning. Fetch 'em out!"

Out they were dragged and laid on the grass for a few minutes, "to drain," as someone remarked, then they were brought to their feet and forced once more towards the wagons on the hill-side. I shall never forget the picture they presented as, dripping wet, with ghastly faces, and literally quaking with fear, they were driven onwards by the showmen, and the crowd that followed behind jeered and taunted them. One of the fellows turned and said, "Are you a-going to kill us? Ain't you done enough to us?"

"Not half enough," was the reply. Thereupon the fellow set up a shout of "Murder! Murder!" "Shut it!" said one of the showmen roughly; "save your breath for the next scene. You'll want it then!" So we came up again to the wagons.

One of the latter had extra large wheels, and very quickly two of the prisoners had their clothes torn off them to the waists, and were triced up each to a wheel with arms and legs stretched out. Then four muscular showmen, smocks and vests off, shirt-sleeves rolled up, and carrying new whalebone riding-whips, took their places by the bound men.

"What is it to be?" asked one of the men, as he drew his whip through his fingers and balanced it. "Two dozen!" said my father, who had been addressed. "Make it three dozen! Make it three dozen for all my beautiful chaney ornaments they smashed, the vagabonds!" shrieked an old woman, whose caravan had been wrecked. "Very well, mother," said father curtly, "three dozen it shall be; three dozen for every man jack of 'em. Lay on, boys!"

There was a sudden swish and flash as the whips curled in the air, then two such yells as I had never heard before from human throats. They seemed to paralyse me, and I could not turn my eyes from the scene, though it frightened me. Swish! swish went the merciless whips, rising and falling regularly, the yells of the suffering wretches, echoed by the other prisoners in anticipation of their own: turn, being punctuated by the sound of someone counting the strokes.

At last "thirty-six" was called. Then the two fellows, with their backs purple-striped and bleeding, were cast loose, their wet rags of clothes were thrown at them, and they were told to "Hook it, sharp!" They needed no second bidding, and scurried, staggering, moaning, and cursing, down the hill-side to the road. "Thank yer stars ye've got off as light as 'ee 'ave!" shouted an old man as they went. "Next time you tries such tricks we'll 'ang 'ee! D'ye hear me? We'll 'ang 'ee, sure!"

Six times this scene was repeated, and when the last of the men had disappeared, with smarting back and oath-laden tongue, down the hill, the woman's turn came.

"Carroty Kate" flung many foul words at us as she was unfastened from the wagon wheel and dragged forward, but her face was white – ay, I can see it in my mind even now, after all these years – chalky white, against the tousled mass of red hair that framed it, and she was evidently badly frightened.

"What are you going to do to me?" she raved.

"Give you a lesson same as the men," replied one of the showmen. He was proprietor of a little waxwork booth, I recollect, and his property had suffered badly in the roughs' onslaught. "We're not a-going to drag 'ee through the pond," he continued, "bad as you wants washin', nor use the horse-whips to 'ee, but you're a goin' to be made to smart all the same." And she *was* made to smart.

Some penny canes were brought out, such as were sold in the fair, the virago was forced over a trestle, and two strong young women administered a sound thrashing.

She screamed and swore horribly, and writhed about, so that the half-dozen stout show-women who were holding her had a difficult task. But the young women flogged on till they were tired, and then the red-haired wretch was allowed to limp away, cursing us as she went in the most dreadful fashion. Some others of the fair-wrecking mob also got punished, though not by the showmen. They fell in with a party of police near Bath, and a desperate fight ensued, the officers using the heavy staves with deadly effect on the drink-soddened rioters. Many of the latter, besides being badly mauled, were arrested, and several were transported for breaking the King's peace. I heard in after years, though we knew nothing of it at the time, that one man who maimed a policeman with an iron bar, so that the poor fellow was crippled for life, was sentenced to death, and executed, for "wounding, with intent to kill".

At any rate, an amazing amount of mischief was wrought by the Bath roughs on that occasion at Lansdown Fair, and the night of awful fear they caused us, with the rough justice their leaders met at the hands of my father and his companions, are things that burned into my memory, to remain with every detail fresh and vivid through the whole of my life.

Such scenes are impossible in England now, and for that fact no one is more sincerely thankful than myself. At the same time, looking back upon them, I cannot but feel that the showmen were justified in taking the law into their own hands, and in dealing with those old-time hooligans as they did.

I remember my mother saying as we left Lansdown on that memorable August day for another fair, "Oh, James! It was a terrible beating those Bath people got. I shall never forget it."

They'll remember it longer than you will, my lass, I'll warrant," was father's reply. "Those chaps wanted a lesson written in for 'em so as to keep it in their memories. There's nothing a rough is so careless about as the skin of other people, nothing he is so careful about as his own. Touch his skin and you touch his conscience, and there's no other way of doing it."

Such were my father's sentiments in regard to dealing with that worst of all brutes, the human one, and I have heard him express them many a time. I still appreciate their wisdom, though I have lived on into a softer age in which the ordering of corporal punishment even for the most violent robber would arouse a storm of indignation. But it is not for the showman to moralize. I must proceed with my story and leave you to judge the differences existing between my early days and the present ones for yourselves.

# CHAPTER XI

## GRIM TRAGEDY AND LEGAL FARCE

IN old age – perhaps as one of its compensations – the memory is able to picture with unusual brightness the scenes of one's very early days. Incidents quite forgotten during youth, amid the strenuous work of middle life, come back with a vivid freshness of detail that is amazing. Because of this I could linger long over the events of my childhood. But I feel that I must hurry on, and bridge as quickly as may be the gulf of the years that lie between the peep-show wanderings with my parents and my start into the world on my own account.

After Lansdown, then, with its wild scenes of riot and showmen's justice, we worked our way to the great fair at Bristol. This commenced always on September 1st, and lasted for ten days. It was held under the shadow of the glorious old church, on ground a portion of which is now the Haymarket, and a charge of a guinea a foot was levied for the frontage of each show or stall, the money going to the clergy of St. Mary Redcliffe.

At this fair I was to get another tragic experience, one which, incidentally, though without reason, was made for a time to reflect adversely on the poor show-folk generally.

One of the biggest shows at the fair was Middleton's Theatre. The proprietor, Charles Middleton, eldest of three brothers, all famous as showmen – two in the dramatic, and one in the marionette line – aimed at making his establishment as noted as Richardson's was, and to this end spared no expense in regard to talent.

This season he had secured as his leading man an actor named Bartlett, a man of exceptional ability, who had gained a great reputation not only in the provinces, but on the London stage.

Bartlett had married a smart young woman who was a very talented actress, and she had been engaged to play with her husband. She was born in a village just outside Bristol, and when the pair arrived for the September fair, her mother, a widow in good circumstances, came into the town to see her daughter and to witness her theatrical performances.

Early the next morning, which was Sunday, it was bruited about that Mrs. Bartlett's mother had been found brutally murdered in a field not far from the little farm she occupied. There was tremendous excitement in Bristol when the news became known, and all the show people, my father, my brother William, and myself amongst them, walked out to view the scene of the tragedy. Middleton's people, of course, went, and with them Bartlett and his wife, both of them seemingly broken down with grief at the terrible fate of the old lady.

We all visited the spot where the body had been found, with the head partly shot away. Then we made our way back towards Bristol, Bartlett returning with the party, but leaving his wife with friends in the village.

At a roadside inn, not far from the city, all stopped for refreshment, the crowd filling the large tap-room, the crime being the sole topic of conversation as the drinks were served. All at once one of the tap wenches – there were no stylish barmaids in those days – stopped in front of Bartlett, who was sitting on a settle near the fireplace, and said, "Why, you're the man who came in late last night with the woman who has been found murdered!"

There was a pretty commotion at this, I can tell you. Bartlett called the girl a fool, and said that he had not been out of Bristol till that morning. But the girl persisted, saying, "I know it was you. I knew you directly I saw you, from the way you carry your head!"

The actor had a trick of carrying his head slightly on one side, the result being to give him a somewhat swaggering appearance, and that was what the girl alluded to. In the end, though he strenuously denied that he had ever been in the house before, Bartlett was arrested by a constable who had been fetched, was taken to Bristol, and committed to prison.

All through the fair controversy raged strongly as to his guilt or innocence, and Middleton had to close his theatre, because the country people, always ready to believe that show-folk were little better than criminals, threatened to wreck the place. None of us did well after the discovery of the murder, and we were glad to get away from Bristol, Bartlett being still in prison when we left.

The crime was eventually brought home to him, news of his trial, confession, and execution reaching us a month later at Wantage fair. It appears that Bartlett discovered that his wife, on her mother's death, would be entitled to a nice sum of money, and when the old lady visited them at Bristol fair he resolved to hasten her end. After the show closed he slipped out without being noticed, waylaid his mother-in-law, who, in the presence of some of the company, had previously bidden him and her daughter "Good-night," and shot her with a pistol – one of the stage properties he had loaded for the purpose.

There were many people who did not hesitate to say that Mrs. Bartlett knew what her husband's intentions were towards her mother on that fatal Saturday night. In such cases, however, the world is always censorious, and in those days it was always ready to believe anything bad of show-folk. The poor woman, however, did not live very long after the tragedy, her heart, my father always declared, being broken by the unjust suspicions entertained against her.

Bartlett's crime caused many innocent persons, besides his wife, much bitter trouble and suffering. For a very long time afterwards, particularly in the West of England, show-folk, more especially strolling players, were continually taunted as "murderers". In one or two places they were actually driven away, and their shows wrecked by mobs who shouted, "Down with the play-actors who killed the poor old woman!"

Nor were the authorities over-ready to give aid or justice to strollers even when the latter were shown to be right in their demands for assistance. Many persons looked upon van-dwellers and showmen quite as the "rogues and vagabonds" they were dubbed in earlier days, and treated them accordingly. A vivid memory of what happened to ourselves in this connection is with me to this day.

We had our peep-show at Uphaven, a little place about ten miles from Devizes; and famous for its big October cattle and hiring fair. Like Lansdown it attracted a lot of roughs, who after the fair was over amused themselves by destroying the showmen's property. We finished early in the evening, packed up, and took our caravan to a piece of waste land some hundred and fifty yards from the last house in the village. Here, after a hasty supper, we went to bed, all lights being put out, so as not to attract the mischievous attention of the roughs who were prowling about.

All went well until about three in the morning, when we were aroused by banging of cudgels on the side of our wagon. Smash! smash! smash! went the big sticks, to the ruin of the gaily-painted panels in which we took much innocent pride. My little sister screamed with fear, and we boys were badly frightened, though we did not cry out. Father got out of bed and reached for his blunderbuss, which on this occasion had a handy marble dropped into it instead of a bullet.

The fellows outside, who must have numbered nearly a dozen, evidently heard him moving, and rushing to one side of the caravan, caught hold of the wheels and turned it completely over.

My, what a crash that was! Pots and pans, cups and saucers, came clattering about us as we were thrown higgledy-piggledy out of bed, frantic with fright, all bruised, and some of us badly cut by the glass from the broken windows. Father, however, had not dropped the blunderbuss, and as the caravan, luckily, was thrown over with the side-door uppermost, he managed to open it and get outside.

As soon as they had turned our van over the ruffians had rushed laughing down the road. But they had not got too far for a pot-shot, and dad let fly after them. Bang! went the old blunderbuss, like a young cannon, and a loud yell told us that the marble had found its mark. Then all was silent save for a clattering of heavily booted feet that soon died away in the distance.

Father pulled mother and the rest of us out of the overturned wagon, and we shivered in the chilly morning while he went to get some help to put our van upright again. Some of his showmen friends were soon on the spot, and the caravan having been put on its wheels we started to put things to rights as well as we could, and to make ourselves as comfortable as possible till daybreak.

When that came it was seen that it would cost several pounds to make good the damage that had been done. It was a dreadful calamity for us, for we were very, very poor just then, and father swore that those who had committed the wanton act should feel the weight of the law. But in doing this he had not reckoned on the prejudice against the poor show-folk and the pigheadedness of country magistrates.

Full of his intention to bring our assailants to justice he set to work, and soon found that a certain man had been medically treated for a wound in his back, from which a marble had been extracted. So he got the village constable to arrest the fellow, who was brought before the nearest justice.

The latter, however, happened to be the man's master, and at once showed where his sympathies lay. The court room was the vestry of the church, and a good many people, including the parson of the parish, were present to hear my father lay his complaint.

"Pooh!" said the J.P., "pooh!" when my father had stated his case. "This man works for me and is one of my best farm-hands. He wouldn't do such a thing, and I don't believe a word you say. You vagabonds of showmen would tell any lie. As for the wound, that was caused by an accident in getting over a fence!"

Father was too astounded to answer him, and at once saw what sort of "justice" he might expect, when the parson got up and said that he, too, was quite sure the charge was a mistaken one, even if it was not deliberately false.

"The man comes regularly to church," said the cleric, "and I am sure he had nothing to do with the attack on this fellow's caravan. No doubt the mischief was done by some of the showmen themselves!"

"Of course it was," said the magistrate; "of course it was!" Then he turned to my father and said, "You be off! And don't you come here again. If you're caught trespassing anywhere I shall know what to do with you. Be off! be off!"

Father came away a very angry man, and I know mother had much ado to quiet him down. For years afterwards Uphaven had only to be mentioned, and my poor old dad would launch into a tirade against the treatment he had received there, and the iniquity of allowing the law to be administered by prejudiced and ignorant country squires, such as the one he appeared before.

Thank God! I have lived to see more generous days; days in which justice is evenly administered to rich and poor alike: days, too, in which the once despised mummer and the showman win not merely appreciation from a kindly public to whose entertainment they devote their lives, but high honour and position in the State.

In this respect I personally have much to be grateful for. Our late revered Queen Victoria and our present noble King have overwhelmed me with their gracious kindliness. Nobody would have imagined – least of all my poor father and mother – that the little travelling show-boy would ever come to be honoured by his country's rulers, both by kindly speech and Royal letters.

Having been led away by my thought of the contrast between those old days and the present ones, you must pardon me if I still further digress to mention his Majesty's latest kindness to me. I am anxious to publish in this account of my life some letters I had received from Queen Victoria, couched in the most kindly and informal terms. So I wrote to King Edward and asked his permission to publish the letters in question. At once I received a reply, asking me to forward them for the King's perusal before granting my request. I did so, and with very little delay received them back again, carefully registered, from Buckingham Palace, together with a note from Lord Knollys, saying that the King had commanded him to inform me that his Majesty had no objection to my making them public. The incidents that called them forth I must deal with in their proper place, but I give you the letters here because they will help my readers to appreciate an old man's feelings of wonder and gratitude on contrasting, as I have done just now, the attitude adopted towards showmen in the old days with that accorded in these more enlightened times.

Here is one I received after a performance at Balmoral, where her Majesty displayed such graciousness that I could not help telegraphing to Sir Arthur Bigge how honoured and grateful I was for the kindness shown to me and mine:–

BALMORAL,
June 19th, 1898.
DEAR SIR, When your telegram arrived last evening I was about to write, by command of the Queen, to thank you for the ready willingness in which your manager met her Majesty's wishes to see your circus, and also for the pair of Shetland ponies presented in your name to her Majesty. The Queen was very sorry that owing to a mistake application for the circus to come here was not made until it had left Ballater, which her Majesty fears must have entailed much extra trouble and fatigue. I have further to express the thanks of the Queen for the kindly and loyal sentiments contained in your telegram. I am forwarding to Mrs. Sanger from the Queen a small souvenir of Friday's performance, which her Majesty witnessed with much interest and satisfaction.
Yours faithfully,
ARTHUR BIGGE.

A year later I received a letter from Balmoral from the Queen's private secretary asking when I was likely to be in the neighbourhood of Windsor Castle, as the Queen would like to see my circus again. I duly replied, and the performance took place on Monday, July 17th, 1899. The Queen was particularly interested in the elephants, asked me their names and many questions about them. The result was that when the tragic affair happened at the Crystal Palace in February 1900, and my elephant, "Charlie," killed a man who had been teasing him, I received, to my grateful astonishment, the letter which appears in Chapter 42. Can you wonder that I am proud and grateful for such recognition, when I remember what my struggles were in those past days, whose story, having thus digressed, I must now hasten to resume?

# CHAPTER XII

## HOW FATHER SAVED MY LEG

AS TIME went on I grew very tall and strong, thanks to the active life of the road: in the winter carrying on our fish and vegetable trade, in the summer and the early autumn journeying from fair to fair with our roundabout and peep-show. I was ambitious to become an acrobat, and in my spare time steadily practised the various feats of performers I had seen at the fairs, until I became, for a youngster, quite proficient in the minor branches of the art, such as somersaults and balancing tricks.

Father used to encourage me in this practice. "Learn all you can, my boy," he would say; "the poorest trick may come in useful some day, if it is only that of knowing how to tumble down without hurting yourself. If you do hurt yourself, remember, "well endured is half cured."

That advice has helped me often, both in bodily and financial tumbles, and of these I have had many, some of them very severe ones, in my long career. There was another saying of my father's that I have never forgotten, to the effect that "the worst always happens to the man who is ready to believe the worst." This was said in circumstances that deeply impressed me not only mentally but physically, for the marks will go with me to my grave.

The incident occurred some two years after the big events I have been relating, when I had grown to be a strong and fearless boy. We were at a small fair in Kent, in the Romney Marshes, and I was looking after the roundabout. I have related how this machine was constructed, and how its motive power came from the lads of the village, who would push it round in return for an occasional free ride.

I was so used to it that I was accustomed to walk on the spars that carried the horses and the riders, even when the roundabout was going at its fastest pace. Custom, no doubt, made me careless. Anyhow, on this particular occasion as I went to do something at the centre of the machine, which worked on a pivot in a kind of open trunk, my foot slipped, my right leg was jammed between the pivot and the spars, and in a moment a bolt literally tore the flesh of the calf away from the limb. There was a loud scream on my part, and then for the first and only time in my life I fainted. Father heard the cry and quickly saw what had happened. He at once wound some strips of canvas about my leg – we wore knee-breeches then – and fetching a horse, put me in front of him on the saddle and rode off to seek a doctor.

It was a three-mile journey, and when we did find a surgeon he gave me something to drink, looking at the wound, and immediately told my father that the limb must come off. Father protested against this idea, and another surgeon was called in for consultation. He agreed with his colleague that the leg must come off, otherwise I should die, because the injury was so great, the flesh so torn, that it was bound to mortify. Even if I did have my leg off they would not guarantee to save my life. Such operations were dangerous things at that time. There were no anaesthetics or antiseptics, and the shock to the patient of the surgeon's knife and saw was always a terrible one.

I remember hearing the discussion as if in a dream. I was in no pain, only very faint, with a predominant feeling of curiosity, which I can vividly recall, as to how I should look with a wooden leg, and what my friends would think of me. Then suddenly I heard my father say, "By the honour of God!" (This was the only oath I ever heard from his lips, and when he uttered it he always made it a solemn obligation.) "By the honour of God! whether the boy lives or dies it shall be with all his limbs on him. If you can't help him, I must see what I can do myself!"

With that, he pulled the bandages together over the injury, picked me up off the doctor's couch, put me on the horse again, and rode back as fast as possible to the fair and our caravan. Here in our little living room he laid me down, told mother to go outside and not be frightened, and then with a curved needle and some thick white silk thread sewed the torn calf back into its position.

Sixteen stitches were put into that wound in good sailor fashion, and as father did the work he kept saying, "Don't halloa, it'll soon be finished! Be a man, Georgie!" So I did my best not to whimper, though I couldn't help grinding my teeth, and was very glad when I saw him put that big curved needle down.

When the stitching was complete, father finished the job with a strapping of diachylon plaster, of which we always carried a good supply; then he put me to bed and told me to lie still. From that time onward, though it ached now and again, my leg began to get well, but it was not till six weeks had passed that I was able to walk about again.

When I did begin to move I soon recovered my activity, and from that day to this the limb which the doctors said must come off has served me well and given me no trouble. The long stitches are still there to view, and many a medical man who has seen them has expressed the opinion that my father, either by wonderful skill or wonderful good luck, succeeded in performing a really marvellous bit of surgery.

That I did not become a cripple with a crutch and a timber toe, and with most of my chances in life spoilt thereby, I owe entirely to the self-reliance and resource of that brave old sailor-showman father of mine.

The next great change in my life that I remember was when we left Newbury to make London our abiding place when we were not on the road. The cause of our leaving the Berkshire town where I first saw the light, and that I love so well, was father's determination not to submit to what he considered injustice.

The tax-collector called for the taxes, making a demand for two amounts at the same time. "No," said father, "only one tax is due and only one will I pay. When the other tax is due you shall have the money."

"Oh," said the collector, "we can demand the tax that is not due beforehand if we want it. The town is poor, and we need money badly; you must pay what I demand." "I will not do anything of the sort," replied my father. "Very well," said the collector, "then you will be made to pay!" And with that he went off.

The next thing was that father was served with a summons, and directly he got it he walked into the house and ordered us to help him take the furniture into the road. This we did in fear and trembling, but without question, for we knew father. When our belongings were in the street he sent round the bellman to call what was known in those days as a forced sale, and then in the open air sold off everything for what it would fetch.

This done, he went to see the mayor, who kept a draper's shop, and told him that he had now no property that was distrainable for taxes, at the same time complaining bitterly of the way in which they were levied.

"Well, Mr. Sanger," said the mayor, "I'm very sorry you should have been driven to this. But you know this town is just now very poor. We have many people on the rates who won't or can't work, and the industrious must pay for the idle."

"By the honour of God!" shouted father, "if that's Newbury doctrine I'll have no more of it! I will pay no more."

Nor did he. Back he came straightway from his interview with the mayor, locked the door of the house, put the horses into our caravan and wagon, and started with us all on the road again.

We were very grieved to leave Newbury, where we had many friends and playmates, but father's word was law, and away we went. I remember my poor mother saying, as she looked back down the road, "We've had some good times there, James; I shall miss my old neighbours and the four-pin matches. But I suppose you know best, and it's not for me to grieve." That was all; but I noticed her wipe her eyes with her apron several times when father was not looking.

# CHAPTER XIII
## HOW A GIANT DIED

WHEN we reached London after leaving Newbury we made our winter pitch in the Kennington Road, on a piece of waste ground, then known as the Mall. This latter was an enormous space where showmen of every kind came to winter, and the authorities never interfered with them. Those who know the neighbourhood now can scarcely conceive what it was like at that period. There were no shops worthy of the name, but on one side were rows of old wooden huts and stalls from which various wares were sold. On the other side the vans of the showmen covered the great space, for which they paid no rent.

To have paid rent with many of them would indeed have been impossible. Many found only a bare hand-to-mouth living in the summer months, and in winter had to exist as best they could, very often, though helped by neighbours nearly as poor as themselves, literally starving to death. One such case occurred soon after we had taken up our quarters there. The circumstances made it very pathetic, and deeply impressed us at the time.

One of the people who brought his little show to winter on the Mall was an exceptionally tall man, named Thompson, who travelled the fairs as the Scotch Giant. He was of superior education, and was very reserved as to his early history, and, indeed, as to his affairs generally. The summer had not been very prosperous with him, and what little money he had was exhausted early in the winter months. But he would ask nobody for assistance, and strove to earn a few pence by writing letters or business documents for those show-men who were too illiterate to do such things for themselves. There was very little of this work, however, and as the winter advanced things with poor, proud Thompson grew very bad indeed.

At last, on a bitter day in the latter weeks of January, somebody went to Thompson's van with a letter they wished him to read for them. Knocking brought no reply, and the question went round, "Has anybody seen Thompson?" Nobody had. The silence was ominous, and at length a showman who knew him well burst open the caravan door. There upon the bare floor, for he had sold everything that was saleable out of his tiny travelling home, lay the poor Scotch Giant, quite dead. He had been starved to death. It was shown at the inquest that he could have had nothing to eat for days. He was too proud to ask a neighbour for a crust, and in that bitter weather, without fire or covering, had laid himself down, a gaunt, emaciated figure, worn by hunger to a skeleton, and had passed silently away.

Many a time at the fairs I had heard some temporarily engaged helper inviting the public to step up and see "the wonderful Scotch Giant, the tallest man in the world!" "Acknowledged to be," so the patter ran, "the finest specimen of humanity ever brought before the public." Little did I dream that one day I should see this really magnificent man lying, a pitiful bag of bones, dead of starvation, on the floor of his stripped and empty caravan on the wild waste of Kennington Mall!

The irony of the tragedy was made the greater when, only a few weeks afterwards, persons came inquiring Thompson's whereabouts, and it was learned that through the death of a relative in Scotland he had succeeded to a very considerable fortune. At the time of his death, though he knew it not, he was comparatively a wealthy man. And he died of starvation!

Such are the freaks that Fortune plays us, poor puppets that we are, worked by the strings of inexorable circumstance. I was to see many such in my career as a showman, now about to widen out in an unexpected manner, but none has more deeply impressed me than the winter tragedy of the poor Scotch Giant.

# CHAPTER XIV

## HOW THE GIPSIES FOUGHT AT MOULSEY RACES

IN London that winter, after leaving Newbury, we had some very hard times. Our fish and vegetable trade had finished when we left the Berkshire town, and the family had to live on the little father had managed to scrape together as savings. This was not a lot, and we were very glad when the time came for us to take the road again.

We went our usual round, visiting amongst other gatherings Moulsey Races. This river-side meeting was to provide me with another lasting experience, thanks to the rivalry existing between certain families of gipsies.

Now I want to correct here a very popular error – namely, the belief that in those early days the gipsies were showmen, and most of the showmen gipsies. Nothing could be further from the truth. The gipsies, it is true, went from fair to fair, but it was as horse-dealers, hawkers of baskets and tinware, workers of the lucky-bag swindle, fortune-tellers, and owners of knife and snuff-box shies. The showmen proper always kept themselves apart from the gipsies, who invariably camped in a different spot to that occupied by the caravans. I do not think I ever saw genuine gipsies acting as showmen, though I have known them as proprietors of very large drinking and dancing booths. As a matter of fact, the show business was mainly in the hands of the Jews, who in my day outnumbered the Gentile entertainers by two to one, and were always good friends and comrades to us.

But the gipsies, though we kept apart from and, indeed, rather looked down upon them, had the trick of making money, and having made it were very fond of displaying their wealth on their persons in the shape of finery and trinkets. Each tribe or family was always trying to outvie the others in the matter of personal show. Bitter rivalries sprang up between them, and at that time of day there was scarcely a fair or race-meeting that did not end with a savage fight amongst the gipsies.

There were two great occasions on which this rivalry was always conspicuously displayed. These were Fairlop Fair and Moulsey

Races. Fairlop Fair, I may mention, was held in Hainault Forest. It had its origin in a social meeting commenced by Daniel Day, a noted ship's rigging and block maker of Wapping, who used to entertain his friends annually under the famous Fairlop Oak to a feast of broad beans and bacon. At his death he left a sum of money to perpetuate the custom, and in compliment to the founder large parties used to proceed from Wapping on the appointed day in boats placed on wheels and drawn by teams of grey horses, making, with bands of music and banners, quite a brilliant procession. The rendezvous was the spot where the Fairlop Oak had stood, for that venerable tree had disappeared before my day, having been cut down after braving the storms of centuries to make, amongst other articles, the pulpit for the new church of St. Pancras in Euston Square.

This, however, is by the way. What I want you to understand is that this fair, which was always opened by the singing of the song, "The Brave Old Oak," had grown to be a great gathering-place for showmen who went to make a living by amusing the public, and the gipsies, who, in addition to seeking money there, made it the occasion on which to display all their new clothes.

I have seen young gipsy girls – gloriously beautiful some of them were too – literally draped from shoulders to ankles in silk handkerchiefs of the most costly description, great gold bangles on their wrists, heavy jewelled ornaments in their ears, and flashing rings on their fingers, flaunting their finery at this fair in the forest.

With them would walk their chosen gipsy swains, clad in shining velveteen, spangled with buttons of gold, silver, and pearl. Buckles of silver and glittering paste adorned their clog shoes, and peeping from the black, well-oiled locks that hung under the broad felt hats to their shoulders might be seen enormously thick gold ear-rings. They made a brave show, I can tell you, and the Rossiter who out-did a Lee, or a Scampe a Samson in display, or vice versa, did not forget to shower biting taunts upon the discomfited rival, with the result that fierce fights became the order of the day.

Well, Fairlop Fair had come and gone with a more than usually bitter battle between the Lees and the Rossiters. Each party had badly mauled the other, but neither could claim a decisive victory and rumour grew that Moulsey Races would witness another deadly struggle between them. At last it became known on the road that the champion bruisers of the two tribes, Jimmy Lee and Tommy Rossiter, were to meet in properly set battle to decide the mastership. Both men were noted pugilists, and the excitement amongst the showmen at the news was intense. At every stop on the road the coining fight was the one topic of conversation, and betting as to the result was fast and furious.

Father did not bet, but, nevertheless, he took great interest in the event, for, sailor-like, he loved a good stand-up fight with fair play, no favour, and the best man to win. He had taught us boys to use our fists pretty well, and always impressed on us that they were an Englishman's natural weapons, and that only cowards and foreigners used anything else in disputes between man and man. So I was all agog, too, regarding the gipsy battle, and anxiously awaiting its issue.

At last the day arrived, and we found ourselves with peep-show and roundabout at Moulsey Races. It was a tremendous gathering, and the boats that ferried the majority of visitors over the river to the meeting must have taken small fortunes in the shape of fares. The gipsies were there in force, their gay raiment making the moving crowds brilliant with colour. Business was brisk, too, and we did wonderfully well at our pitch, which was on a bit of rising ground looking towards the river.

The Lees had got a pitch with their "shies" down towards the river, and some distance away from them were the Rossiters with a similar establishment. About each party the fair-goers pressed in throngs, and from our position we could see the big sticks – "livetts" they were termed – hurtling towards the knives and snuff-boxes which formed the prizes for skilful shots, and were placed on tall ash rods, stuck into baskets full of mould, ranged against a canvas background. That was before the day of the "roll, bowl or pitch," with a ball, for coco-nuts. The latter were then rather costly rarities, and iron snuff and tobacco boxes, with cheap knives, as I have said, were put up at two shies a penny to tempt onlookers to try their luck with the "livetts." The latter could also be used for quite other and more harmful purposes, as we were soon to see.

About four o'clock the crowd about our pitch thinned down to nothing, and business came to a standstill. The people were all making their way towards a spot near the river, where I could see, from my point of vantage on the top of our roundabout, a ring had been made by the gipsies armed with their heavy "livetts."

Presently a roar went up as two lithe figures stripped to the waist, their bodies shining like old ivory in the summer sunshine, stepped out on the green grass and faced each other. There was a pause.

Then another roar, and as I sat on my perch and trembled with excitement I saw a quick flash of sinewy arms, two jumping, dodging bodies, now close together, now apart again, and knew that the big fight had begun.

How that crowd round the battling men did yell and sway, the ring of brightly dressed gipsies keeping a clear space for the combatants with their swinging "livetts." I yelled and shouted with the rest as the pugilists dashed at each other with their iron fists, jabbed, countered, closed, and broke away, each grimly determined not to yield to the other as long as he could stand upon his legs. A brutal sight, you may say; but, oh, the excitement of it!

I suppose some five punishing rounds had been fought when there came from the crowd about the ring a mightier roar than ever. Louder and louder rose the babel of voices, the ring with the struggling men in the centre grew smaller and smaller as the mass of forms swayed hither and thither about it. Then I saw that the gipsies, no longer in a circle, but in a compact body, were battering with their heavy "livetts " at a knot of men who were pushing towards the place where the pugilists still battled. The sun gleamed on a row of hard tall hats. It was the police who had arrived to stop the fight!

They did, so far as the battle of the gipsy champions was concerned, for the ring was broken up, and the pugilists were separated in the jostling, pushing crowd. But another fight infinitely more brutal and damaging was at once in progress. The gipsies, infuriated by their interference, attacked the police, who were very few in number, in the most merciless fashion. Bash! bash! bash! went the heavy "livetts" on tall hats and blue-coated shoulders, as, vainly endeavouring to retaliate with their short batons, the representatives of law and order were driven, many of them streaming with blood, towards the river.

"My God, boy! There will be murder done this day!" said my father, who had climbed on the roundabout to my side, and it certainly looked like it. We saw the police with many of the frightened spectators scrambling towards the two big ferryboats. Behind them pressed the gipsies with those terrible "livetts," beneath which men went down like pole-axed oxen. Still forms were distinguishable here and there on the river-bank stretched out dead or insensible. It was like a battlefield for its action and its clamour, and I shall never forget the scene or the white faces of that other crowd that, deathly still, watched it with ourselves from the vantage place of the showground.

At last, just as the ferry-boats, overladen with fugitives, had sunk and thrown their freight of frightened and wounded men into the river, luckily very shallow at that point, there was a cessation of hostilities almost startling in its suddenness. As if at a signal, the attacking gipsies stopped striking at their beaten foes, and, turning round, made for their camps.

In a few minutes the latter were broken up, and vehicles of all kinds, from donkey-barrows to pairhorse vans, were steaming up the road as hard as they could go, laden with hastily packed dunnage and swarthy owners. They rattled past in a long line that, without any exaggeration, I should say, for my memory of it is very vivid, extended for quite a mile. Lees and Rossiters, Scampes, Samsons, and Fearns were hurrying from the scene of their latest exploits, for fear of what might happen to them in consequence. They were cunning people, whose ways were dark and mysterious. Before anybody else could have known it they were made aware that a big force of armed constables was on its way to Moulsey. The word was passed to the gipsies who were fighting, the melee stopped as if by magic, and then came the sudden flight, which remains with me as one of the most remarkable sights I have ever witnessed.

As it chanced, nobody was killed at that memorable race-meeting, though one or two persons, all policemen, were brought very near to death. Some of the gipsies were later arrested, and I believe a Lee was transported for his share in the battle. That was all. The authorities in those "good old times" were a much more easy-going, non-interfering lot than they are today, and a rougher mannered population took full advantage of the fact.

# CHAPTER XV
## THE GREAT HYDE PARK FAIR

Now I must press on with my narrative, and so come to another event that looms big in my life – the great fair in Hyde Park that was held when Queen Victoria came to the throne. We were on the road on our summer tour when the news reached us – I think it was at Somersham, in Huntingdonshire, just after the June fair – that King William IV was dead, and that our late glorious and revered Queen had succeeded him.

Anyhow, I know that father, with his usual enterprise, set to work, and obtained pictures of the death-bed, the lying-in-state, and the funeral of Britain's sailor King as attractions for our peepshow, and that these were exhibited, and I pattered concerning them with great success, at the various fairs in that year, 1837, till winter came upon us, and we returned to London.

As, of course, my readers are well aware, the coronation of Queen Victoria did not take place till a year after her accession, and this enabled the planning of many great and unusual festivities to mark the wonderful June that witnessed the happy and epoch-making event. Amongst others who planned were her Majesty's loyal showmen, who debated all sorts of schemes during their winter rest, and eventually decided that if leave could be obtained a fair in Hyde Park would prove not the least of London's attractions during the festive month.

Nelson Lee and John Johnson, the then proprietors of the original and famous Richardson's show and the City of London Theatre in Shoreditch; Mr. L. Watkins Williams, a Liveryman of the City, who had a noted restaurant in the Old Bailey and an interest in one of the big menageries; and Mr. Samuel Algar, a "Wine and Porter Merchant," as the style went in those times, of the Mile End Road, took the matter in hand; the Queen was petitioned, and graciously gave permission for the holding of the fair.

The latter, the like of which has never since been seen, lasted for nine days, the original grant of a week having been kindly extended by her Majesty, and attracted all the great exhibitions in the country with a whole army of minor showmen.

Richardson's Theatre was there with all the best actors of the day performing Shakespearean dramas. Wombwell and Hilton rivalled each other with their menageries; circuses, waxwork, marionette, and other shows, the biggest of their kind, bearing such famous names in the fair-going world as Scoughton, Baker, Smith, Webster, Atkinson, etc., took up wide spaces in the vast park. Between them were sandwiched the smaller affairs, such as our peep-show and roundabout, and the freak and curiosity booths with amazing canvases depicting the wonders to be seen within.

I can see those curiosities in my mind's eye now, and a queer collection they were. Giantesses, for instance, were well represented by the Misses Cockayne, described as the American twin sisters. They were fine, tall girls, but as one had one mother and the other another, and their birth place was Whitechapel, their description as "twins" and "American" was just a bit of harmless showman's licence.

Then there were numerous fat men and women, spotted boys, natural and unnatural, fair Circassians, the Hottentot Venus, dwarfs, Miss Scott, the two-headed lady, Yorkshire Jack, the Living Skeleton, and learned pigs and fortune-telling ponies galore.

At this fair, too, there was exhibited almost for the last time a freak that had puzzled and amazed the public for a considerable period. This was Madame Stevens, "the Pig-faced Lady," concerning whom I have one of my promised exposures to make. Madame Stevens was really a fine brown bear, the paws and face of which were kept closely shaved, the white skin under the fur having a close resemblance to that of a human being. Over the paws were fitted white gloves, with well-stuffed fingers, so that the pig-faced lady seemed to have nice plump white arms above them.

The bear was strapped in a chair at the back of the caravan, clothed in female dress, shawl, cap, the poke bonnet of the time, etc. In front was a table at which the seeming lady sat, her paws being laid upon it, and all the rest of the body from the arms of the chair downwards hidden by drapery. Under the table was concealed a boy with a short stick to make the pig-faced lady talk.

When all was ready, and the booth full of spectators, the showman would commence his patter thus, as he pulled aside the curtains:–

"I call your attention, ladies and gentlemen, to the greatest wonder of the world! Behold and marvel! Madame Stevens, the pig-faced lady, who is now in her eighteenth year. I believe that is correct, miss?" (Here the hidden boy would prod the bear, who gave a grunt.) "As you see, ladies and gentlemen, the young lady understands what is said perfectly, though the peculiar formation of her jaws has deprived her of the power of uttering human speech in return.

You were born at Preston in Lancashire?" (Another prod and another grunt.) "Quite so. And you enjoy good health and are very happy?" (Another prod and grunt.) "You are inclined, I suppose, as other ladies, to be led by some gentleman into the holy bonds of matrimony?" (Here the boy would give an extra prod, causing the bear to grunt angrily.) "What, no! Well, well, don't be cross because I asked you!"

This would be sure to raise a laugh and expressions of wonder. Then a plate would be passed round to receive contributions "to buy the lady small comforts and luxuries," as the showman said. After this he would conclude as follows:–

"Now, Miss Stevens, you will return thanks to the ladies and gentlemen for coming to see you!" The boy would use his stick and the bear would growl loudly. The doors of the caravan were then thrown open, and as the sightseers poured out the showman would rush to the front, shouting, "Hear what they say! Hear what they all say about Madame Stevens, the wonderful pig-faced lady!"

This show and some others of its class were stopped by the authorities at the following Camberwell fair, and the pig-faced lady became only a memory, lots of people, to their dying day, believing that such a person really existed.

At Hyde Park I wanted to launch out for myself and to do a few acrobatic tricks, so father allowed me to engage myself to Malabar, the juggler and ball-tosser, to patter outside his show and take part in the performance for four shillings a day.

Malabar, who called himself an American, but who was really an Irishman, was a splendidly built man, standing six feet four inches high, and very clever in his business. One of his great feats was to balance a small donkey strapped to the side of a sixteen-rung ladder, using in connection with the performance the well-known phrase, "Tuppence more and up goes the donkey!"

That came about in this way. After the juggling tricks with the knives, bottles, and balls, Malabar would bring out the ladder and the donkey, put a tin plate in the centre of the small arena, and address the audience as follows:-

"If you wish to see the remaining and most remarkable part of the exhibition, I leave it to your generosity to contribute a little more. There is the plate, ladies and gentlemen; don't be afraid of throwing in your money, I shall not be afraid of picking it up!" In response, coppers would be sure to come rolling in. Then, looking at the plate, Malabar would say, "Ah, I see there is so much. If you will make it up to level money, up goes the donkey. Tuppence more, ladies and gentlemen; only tuppence more, and up goes the donkey!" The coppers would be forthcoming, the donkey balanced in the air, and then the show was cleared for another audience.

On the second morning of the fair it was found that somebody had stolen Malabar's donkey. All efforts to recover the animal proved vain, and, so that the show might be kept on, and to avoid grumbling, it was arranged that I should take the donkey's place. I did so successfully once or twice, and was duly balanced in mid-air, at the top of the ladder, on the chin, forehead, shoulder, and arm of the juggler.

But Malabar was given to drink, and business being brisk, and coin abundant, he one day indulged too freely in beer. I did not notice his condition till after my own little performance, and I had started to ascend the balanced ladder. When I did perceive what had happened my nerves gave way just as I was clutching the sixteenth rung. Malabar lost the balance, and down I came, ladder and all, upon the heads of the spectators. The show was broken up for the night, and, in fact, altogether. Malabar drank enormously and did not show again while the fair lasted. Worst of all, I never got the pay l had bargained for, and all my labour, my little tricks, my patter outside, and the risk of my neck inside the booth went unrewarded.

So I went back to father, and for the remainder of the fair assisted in the management of the peepshow. We did splendid business, and had more money in hand than we had managed to get for many a long day when the great fair broke up, and we went on the road again.

Our first pitch was at Windsor Revels, that were held in Bachelor's Acre. The ground was, however, so crowded that we asked for and obtained permission to stand near the market-place facing the Grand Hotel.

Here I pattered about the death-bed, lying-in-state, and funeral procession of the late King to such effect that the money came rolling in. My patter, in fact – and I say it in all humility – seemed quite as big a draw as the pictures themselves. Many a time the gentlemen staying in the hotel would pay for people to see the show so that they might hear young George rattle off the same old tale.

That, however, is by the way, for our pictures were really excellent of their kind, and I must mention their origin if only in justice to the memory of a humble but remarkable genius. This genius was an Irish artist named Jack Kelly, who lived in Leather Lane, High Holborn. He was a very eccentric character, very kindly-hearted, and very much addicted to strong liquor.

But for this weakness I firmly believe Kelly would have made a great name for himself. As it was, he was artist-in-chief to all the showmen on the road, and might have made more money than he did but for the fact that whoever wanted a picture had to coax and keep him from the public-house until it was finished.

His charges were not great. An ordinary peepshow picture, about four feet by two and a half feet, of some notorious crime, with plenty of colour in it, cost three-and-sixpence. A battle-piece, with hundreds of figures in it, cost seven-and-six! And there was plenty of life in his compositions as well as colour, I can tell you, so that their effect behind the glasses was all that could be wished.

Our pictures of King William's death and funeral cost us the price of battle-pieces. "Sure," said Kelly to my father, "it isn't every day that Kings die. It would be a scandalous thing if a Monarch's death-bed didn't equal in cost the killin' of a lot of ignorant sojers! Seven-an'-six each is the price, Mr. Sanger, and divvle a penny less! Moreover, as ye are an ould customer, I'll give ye my word to kape sober till I've finished the set!" That promise did it. The pictures became ours at seven-and-sixpence each, and a grand bargain they proved. Anyhow, the money they gained did much to help me start a show of my own, and so brought me the acquaintance of the girl who was afterwards to become my dear and loving wife.

# CHAPTER XVI

## SOME SHOWS AND STRANGE SUPERSTITIONS

HAVING saved a little money out of what father had given me when the peep-show did good business, and the small presents I received from time to time from patrons who were pleased with my patter, I was very anxious to help my parents, and thought I might manage a new line of business. So I made my start as an animal tamer.

That sounds big, doesn't it? But my start, like the money I had to make it with, was very small indeed. So were my animals. I went to some dealers in what was then known as the Birdcage Walk, in Bethnal Green, and purchased five hen canaries, two redpoles, and six white mice!

That was my troupe, and I soon had it in training. The little creatures were very docile and intelligent, and the redpoles quickly learned to draw and fire a tiny cannon; the canaries to ride in a little coach, walk a tight-rope, and do a sort of quadrille as I whistled; and the mice to climb poles, bring down flags, and other tiny tricks.

It was almost the first exhibition of its kind, though in later years similar shows became very common, and from its first start on the road, which I travelled in company with the peep-show and roundabout of my parents, proved a great success.

The small canvas booth in which I gave my performance soon proved too small for the patronage received, and nearly every week, as we went from fair to fair, a few more yards of cloth and a bit more timber had to be added.

So much in favour was my little show that I was frequently sent for to give exhibitions at private parties, and this always meant good business. Amongst other places we visited that summer, I recollect, was the Isle of Wight, and I was sent for to give a show before a large party at Cowes. There were present with other guests Lord and Lady Baltaugh, General Eden, Viscount St. Vincent, and Lord Hastings and Lady Flora Hastings. I know I took over nine pounds, the biggest sum I had ever then handled in one afternoon for a show, and great was the family rejoicing accordingly.

We went on from place to place, my performing birds and mice being received almost everywhere with approval. I say almost everywhere, for in one or two small villages the little tricks the tiny creatures did were considered, so great was the superstition amongst the ignorant country-folk at that day, to be due to supernatural agencies.

"Them be witch-taught, them be!" exclaimed a bent old farm labourer at one place. "Them be witch-taught, I tell 'ee! I knows, for I 'ave a-had to work in a pleace where a charmer abided and small creeters had to do as she were a-minded they should. A ronk witch she wur to be sure, and them 'as crossed her knowed it, for she could plague cattle 'oonderful. Gipsy-bred she wur, the old varmint, and them as travels the roads knows wur to find her likes, I'll be bound, to put a spell on small creeters to suit their own purposes. They things be witch-taught, I tell 'ee, and them as is wise'll 'ave nowt to do with 'em."

This was the sort of talk, as nearly as I can reproduce it, to which the ancient gaffer treated a crowd of open-mouthed rustics; and, amazing as it may seem to us now, it impressed his listeners deeply – so much so, in fact, that they took his advice, and had "nowt to do wi' us."

People in these times have no idea of the superstition then prevailing, even amongst the better-class villagers. Witches and warlocks were very real beings to many of them, and Satan was supposed to take an active personal interest in the business of blighting crops, spoiling brews of beer or cider, turning milk sour, laming and killing cattle, and various other misdeeds credited to unfortunate persons whose outward marks of evil were all too often only age, poverty, and lonely wretchedness.

No wonder, then, that the showman and the conjurer were occasionally, to their loss and sorrow, credited with being genuinely in league with the Evil One. An example of this, apart from the instance I have related in regard to my performing birds and mice, was afforded that very same season.

We had travelled to the Michaelmas fair at High Wycombe, where there was always a big gathering of showmen, amongst them on this occasion being Na Barno Eagle with his "Temple of Magic." Eagle, who had been an officer in the British Army, was a clever conjurer, and was considered one of the most dignified showmen of his day. He was very tall, had a majestic manner, a commanding way of talking, could assume a most mysterious air, and, dressed with sombre richness in black velvet, looked the necromancer to perfection. With him assisting in the business, though quite a girl, was his clever, goodlooking daughter Georgiana, who made good use of her father's training in later life, and will still be remembered by many persons as the celebrated Madame Card.

With her Na Barno Eagle performed a bit of thought-reading hanky-panky, a very crude and simple exhibition as compared with the elaborate performances of today, but at that time quite a novelty, and to the simple country-folk alarmingly mysterious.

Anyhow, after Eagle had given one or two performances, the people began to gather in groups and look suspiciously towards his show. Then an old grey beard solemnly averred that the tall man in black was "a true warlock and a servant o' Satan." The old man's words spread from group to group of fairgoers, and at last not a single soul would enter Na Barno Eagle's booth. The old showman tried every possible trick to get the people in, but it was of no use; nobody would enter the "Temple of Magic". Muttered threats, too, were heard as the day went on of ducking the wizard and burning his show, and matters became so threatening that Eagle, long before the fair was over, thought it wise to pack up and clear out.

It must not be thought, however, that all the superstition was confined to the country people. The show-folk had a very fair share also. They believed, or at least some of them did, in signs, omens, and ghostly visitants; so much so, in fact, as on one occasion to make me a witness of a man's hair being turned white through fright. This was at Witney, in Oxfordshire, and the facts, strange as they may seem, are beyond dispute.

We had been to the July fair held in Wychwood Forest, and amongst other showmen was the celebrated Jack Clark, who had one of the best travelling waxwork shows of the day. As at some other fairs I have mentioned, the roughs were always in force at Wychwood, and we therefore all closed our shows early and made our way to Witney. In the principal inn there we all forgathered for rest and refreshment, and in the big room on this occasion some forty or fifty persons were assembled.

Most of them sat at a long table smoking churchwarden pipes, drinking ale, and conversing, the sole illuminant in the great room being a solitary tallow candle in a tin candlestick set in the middle of the table.

Before Jack Clark and two or three of his people was a two-handled half-gallon earthenware pot with ale in it, this being passed from one to another at intervals. Suddenly in the dim light, made dimmer by the smoke of many pipes, there appeared a very tall, cadaverous, gipsy-looking fellow dressed in black. Nobody had noticed his entrance, yet everybody's attention was at once drawn to him.

Without a word the stranger, going behind Clark's chair, reached over, picked up the big pot of ale, and saying, "To our long acquaintance, Jack!" took a pull that nearly emptied the pot, and set it down again.

At this Clark, who was an immensely powerful man, with a great curly mop of brown hair, jumped up in a rage, crying, "Who be you a-drinking my ale like that? I never saw you afore, you black thief!" and struck a blow at the fellow. As he did so the light went out, and when another one was obtained it was seen that the candle was completely reversed in the candlestick, while the tall, dark man had disappeared.

The door of the room was fast shut, nobody had heard it open or close, none of the people sitting by it had noticed anybody pass them. The man had certainly vanished, but how not a soul could tell. After various expressions of wonder the suggestion was made that the strange visitor was the devil himself in person. "If it was," I remember my father saying in a joking way, "he's got a rare taste for ale, eh, Jack!"

But Clark, who was deathly pale, only shook his head. He evidently, strong man as he was, believed fully in the supernatural character of his visitant. So, too, did many of the other showmen, though they rallied Clark on the subject, but without getting any reply save a shake of the head again. Eventually, without uttering another word, the big man, trembling like a leaf, got up, left the room, and went straight to his living-wagon, where he had a nice family.

Here he went off to bed, nor did he get up again for over a week, a doctor being in attendance all the time. When he did reappear amongst us his hair, as luxuriant as ever, was as white as the driven snow. So it remained all his life, for he lived to be a very old man, and at seventy years of age rode at a benefit that was given him at Mrs. Potter's little circus in the New Cut, Lambeth, and did the trick – a very difficult one, by the way – of throwing up a marble and catching it in the neck of a glass bottle. The old man had to be assisted on to the horse by his groom, Bob Archer, who came from Chesham, and was with me afterwards for nine years as stud-groom. Once on horseback, however, Clark showed that he had lost none of his old skill, and his performance was long talked about in Lambeth. His family were long amongst the best artists known in the circus profession, and some of his grandchildren are at present riding in Russia.

Neither I nor my father could ever account for the mysterious affair at Witney, though we always believed it to be a joke played on Clark. But the latter to the day of his death would never speak about it, and always dismissed any attempt to discuss it by saying, "There's some things 'tis best never to think about nor mention."

Such are some of the instances of the superstition prevailing in the days of my youth. I mention them to show what a change in the mental attitude of the public has come about in regard to these things – a change at which no one more heartily rejoices than myself.

As I have said, my show grew rapidly in size and popularity, and I began to help my parents to such an extent that father was able to add "riding" or "over-and-over" boats, as they were called, to his peep-show and roundabouts. In addition to my birds and mice, I got two hares off the Carnarvon estate at Newbury, and taught them to do some very novel tricks with hoops and drums. These also proved a great draw, and we did very well – so much so as to excite the envy of the other show-folk, who in the course of twelve months produced numerous copies of my exhibition.

# CHAPTER XVII

## I TURN COSTER AND FIGHT A BULLY

WE also had some very bad times still, as well as some very good ones. We wintered at this time in a big yard attached to the "King Harry" public house in the Mile End Road, where cattle were brought weekly from all parts of the country for Friday's market at Old Smithfield. A terrible winter it was, with an unusually long spell of hard frost. Our funds in hand were not very heavy, and seeing all our cash going out and none coming in made me very unhappy. At last, however, I struck a new line with considerable success. Wandering on to Bow Common and Hackney Marshes I found numbers of people sliding and skating on the large ponds there. They were trying to keep warm in the bitter weather, and I noticed that, despite the crowds gathered there, nothing was being sold or hawked.

That gave me an idea. I knew how to make rock and toffee, such as was sold at the fairs, for I had assisted in the process many times. Here was my chance. I went and bought about ten pounds of coarse moist sugar, at that time sevenpence a pound, and some oil of peppermint, borrowed some pans to boil it in, and very soon had a nice little stock of strong, good-looking peppermint rock. Then I took it to Hackney Marshes near the biggest piece of ice, and at a penny a lump it sold like wildfire. I was cleared out in an hour, and had made several shillings profit.

I could see I had hit on a good thing, and at once went to work on a bigger scale. I borrowed what little money my brothers William and John had saved, added my stock to it, and then went and purchased a big parcel of sugar from a grocer in the Whitechapel Road and more oil of peppermint.

This I boiled into rock, which was cut into penny lumps, and having pressed my brothers William and John into the service we started out. The rock sale proved as brisk as ever, and we came home with our pockets loaded with coppers and silver, having made over two pounds profit.

The problem of how to live through the winter in London without trenching on the savings from the summer show business, savings that were always needed to give a good start to the caravans when the time came for the road again, was solved.

It was during this winter that I dropped in for the only deliberate battle with my fists I ever took part in, though, as I think I have mentioned before, I could use my hands very well, thanks to my old dad's tuition, if I was attacked. I mention the incident because it helps to emphasize the difference between those days and these, even if it is only in the matter of public-house management.

I was in the taproom of the "King Harry" one night, when a poor, feeble old man came in, who was known as "Gingerbread George," because he was a hawker of gingerbread. He was a harmless old chap, well over seventy, known and respected by all van-dwellers and fair-goers. He gave us "Good evening," and sat down by the fire, putting his hawking basket by his side. His mug of ale had been drawn for him, and he sat sipping it when a fellow named Ned Brumley, came in. Brumley, who was about twenty-five, never did any regular work, and was a bit of a terror in his way, being a drunken bully with some reputation as a boxer. As he lounged in the first thing he did was to kick poor old "Gingerbread George's" basket out of his way, sending the contents all over the place. Naturally the old man protested, and one word led to another, till at last Brumley threatened to smash the old chap's face in. My blood had been boiling for some time, and at this I could stand it no longer, so I jumped up, put myself between the two, saying, "No you won't, Brumley; not while I'm here!"

"You" he said, "you'll stop me; why, I'll–," and in very variegated language he announced that he would smash me and the old man up together, with any other man in the room that dared to interfere. As he yelled out in came the landlord, old Packwood, to learn what the row was about. He was a typical Boniface, was Packwood – such a one as you read about nowadays, but very rarely see. A stout man, with a jolly, round red face, always in his shirt-sleeves and wearing a short white apron. I can picture him now as he stood in that room as plainly as if he were before me in the flesh.

Like most landlords in those days he was a good sportsman, and directly he knew the cause of the quarrel he turned round sharply to me and asked, "Will you fight him, Sanger?"

I'd sooner have died than have drawn back then, so, though I felt uncomfortably dubious as to the result of the encounter, I said, "Yes, I'll fight him." "Good," said Packwood; "get stripped then, you two, while we clear the room," and in a minute he and the customers – there were about twenty present – were piling the tables, settles, and forms round the walls so as to leave a clear space in the middle of the floor.

Just as all was ready in came my brother William, and seeing what was afoot got to my side and whispered, "You're in a mess here, George, if you don't look out. Hit for his body all the time, never mind his ugly face, hit for his body!"

It was sound advice, and I took it, for I was hard as nails, while Brumley was bloated with drink. We faced each other under the swinging oil lamps that lit the room, the sand on the brick floor gritting under our shoes as we moved, and with the word from old Packwood, "Get at it!" at it we went.

The fight didn't last long, but quite as long as I wanted it to do at the pace, for we wasted very little time in sparring. I was lucky at the start. Brumley came for me with a rush and aimed a blow at my head that if I hadn't ducked would have knocked me senseless. But in doing so, he laid himself open for a return, and remembering Brother Bill's advice, I got a twister well home under his ribs that sent him grunting and staggering across the bricks.

That blow no doubt won the battle for me. Brumley came again and again, but with nothing like the fury of the first rush, though once or twice when I was slow in dodging he made me see fireworks. I never aimed once at his head, but pegged away at his body, getting in at length a swinging blow on what old pugilists called the "mark," a point just about where the third button of the waistcoat usually falls. Brumley doubled up like a shut knife, and the fight was over. I lasted six rounds, as I afterwards understood, though I do not remember any appreciable breathing space between them. Anyhow, I had beaten the bully of the neighbourhood, and old Packwood, picking him up and shaking him, pitched him out of doors, and told him never to come into his house again. Then he invited me to have a pint of ale to celebrate the victory, and afterwards set to work to put the taproom once more in order.

Think of a publican in these days, with Brewster Sessions to face, acting as old Packwood did, and inviting and assisting at a fight in his own tap room! His licence would stand a poor chance of renewal. But I want to bring home to you the sweeping character of the social changes that have taken place since I was a stripling, and the incident – though, perhaps, not much to my credit – may help me to do so.

What I personally most dreaded after the fight was facing father and mother, and I crept very sheepishly up the yard and into the caravan. But it was not nearly such an ordeal as I imagined it would be. They had heard all about it, and shook their heads at me as I entered. Then mother fussed about my bruised face with some lotion, while father said dryly, "Well, George, you're going the right way to get the Sangers a name for blackguardism, I hear! Nice goings-on, fighting with a ruffian like Brumley in a public-house. I'm glad you beat him, though, all the same. If you hadn't you'd have got a good hiding from me on top of the other one, and serve you right! Keep out of such things in future, and now get your supper." So it ended, as far as father was concerned, but I have never forgotten the affair nor the way he treated it. After all, if views of life were different then and times were rougher, they were not unwholesome, and made – I venture to think – for manliness. That, however, is only a matter of opinion, and I must get on with my story.

# CHAPTER XVIII

## A CONJURER AT LAST

THOUGH I had gone into the coster trade to help carry things along, I did not neglect my show business that winter. I resolved to take up the "hanky-panky," as the conjuring was called, with the coming season, for I had always a fancy for it from the time I first witnessed the show of a man named Bill Bright, who was one of the oldest fair-goers on the road.

Bill was a West of England man, and he travelled with a mixed exhibition of a sort that in these days, I fancy, has entirely passed away. For instance, one of the items of his show was the "Cackler Dance," in which a girl, apparently tightly blindfolded – I say apparently, for the blindfolding was really only a pretence in order to enhance the ingenuity of the dancer – would do a quick-step amongst a lot of eggs without breaking them. The eggs, about twenty in number, were placed about two feet apart from each other, and the performer, Bill Bright's daughter, would trip the light fantastic, without touching a shell, to the sound of the Pandean pipes.

After the first dance Mrs. Bright, who did the patter in the show, would ask some gentleman amongst the spectators to lend her his watch for a few minutes. Then the borrowed timepiece was placed amongst the eggs, the girl would be handed a big stick, the Pandean pipes would shrill out a lively tune, and a dance of seemingly the most furious character would commence in which the banging of the big stick alternated with the taps of the dancer's heels and toes amongst the eggs.

As the dance proceeded, and the step grew faster, the mother would cry out, "Mind the watch, my dear! Be careful of the gentleman's beautiful watch!" so increasing the excitement of the spectators, especially that of the watch-owner, who soon became filled with alarm for the safety of his property. It was really a most effective show, the nimble dancer making an amazing clatter, till all at once feet and music would stop dead. Then the mother would say, "There you are, ladies and gentlemen, the quickest dance on earth, yet not an egg broken or a scratch upon the gentleman's watch! The young lady now has the privilege of going round to collect what the company may be pleased to give her, after which we shall introduce to you our wonderful display of mystery and magic."

Bill Bright was the "Professor of Magic," and was really a very smart conjurer as things went then. As a boy I was often in his show, and when he asked for juvenile assistants from the audience I would go on to the platform. So I picked up many a wrinkle, noticed the make of the conjuring appliances and steadily practised palming, passing the cards or "slipping the broads," as it was known in the profession, until I felt confident of success.

Intending to become a conjurer, then, I made some cardboard patterns of the trick vases, etc., and took them to a tin-worker in Petticoat Lane, who very soon made the apparatus from my designs. Then I took a large furniture warehouse at the corner of Dog Row, now the Bethnal Green Road, decorated it up, and opened my show. In conjunction with the conjuring and the performing birds and mice I introduced the *poses plastiques*. Madame Walton was then in London giving her living groupings, and very grand they were. I went in for humbler tableaux, depicting Cruikshanks's illustrations of "The Bottle", and the people took to them amazingly. The crowd sometimes was so great that we had to square the policeman not to interfere. My assistants – six young girls, four young men, and two little boys out of the Mile End Road – who had never done anything in the business before, improved in skill nightly, and at last I felt ready to make the first big venture of my life as a showman.

# CHAPTER XIX

## I START A SHOW OF MY OWN

OUR success at the corner of Dog Row having been so marked, I suggested to my brothers William and John, who were my partners in the venture, that we should make it a regular travelling exhibition. They at once fell in with the idea on condition that I made myself the responsible principal of the combination. As John put it, "You do the conjuring and look after the entertainment generally; Will can look after the money-taking and the painting and fitting that may be needed; I'll look after the front, see to the audience, and whip the boys off the steps." So it was arranged, and no brothers ever worked more amicably together.

A man named Bussell fitted up the show-front. We found the canvas, he did the framework, carpentry, and painting, and trusted to our honour to pay him. I have often said since then, "God bless that man!" for he enabled us to start in style without expending our little stock of ready money.

Father and mother were pleased to think we were about to make a start for ourselves on such a grand scale. "I suppose," he said, as he looked at me with a twinkle in his eyes, "his 'lordship' schemed it out?" He always used to call me "his lordship" because I was a bit of a dandy in my way at that period, and, in fact, had gained the nickname amongst the show-folk of "Gentleman George." I suppose I was a somewhat vain youngster; or I was not a bad-looking chap, so the girls at least led me to think, since more than one had set her cap at me, and I liked to dress up to the idea.

After all, pride in one's personal appearance is not a bad thing, provided it isn't carried so far as to become overweening conceit. Smart looks count for much in this world, and to a showman, as I have long since discovered, are simply invaluable.

I accordingly intended in my new business to cut a dash, and many were the colloquies in the family caravan as to the style of dress I should adopt. At last, after much debate with mother and several female friends, it was decided that nothing would be so suitable for "Young George's" style of beauty as a Hamlet costume.

That being settled, they set to work, and very soon I had a fine black velvet tunic, trimmed with black bugles, which at that time were very scarce and expensive. My hat, also of black velvet, carried three nice ostrich feathers, and my Hessian boots had four inches of black velvet round the tops, trimmed with black beads, with bunches in front to form the tassels. In this garb, with a large white turn-down collar and white linen cuffs, and my long hair manipulated with the curling-tongs, I was indeed a showman dandy!

Some of this finery came to me as presents, for, as I have said, all the girls were on my side. The collars and cuffs were made for me by a girl named Anne Hartley, who was a collar-maker. Some of the beads came from a pretty girl who was well known in the Mile End Road as "Watercress Betty." She made a good living by hawking the wholesome tea-table salad, and more than once evidenced that she was not indifferent to my personal charms. I was yet to meet my fate, so her advances were quite thrown away.

Another admirer sent me some sash ribands. This was a widow named Miller, years older than myself, but still comely and buxom. Her husband had been in the small marionette line, and with her sons she still carried on the business, and was wintering with the rest of us in the "King Harry" yard.

These feminine attentions were very flattering to your humble servant, though they awakened no responsive chord of love. I accepted them, because they were pressed upon me, and favoured none of the ladies more than another. Naturally, I was polite and agreeable to them, but that was all, my dear readers, I assure you.

But this boldly-exhibited affection for me led to unpleasant consequences. The widow's two sons each threatened to give me a good hiding if I dared to marry his mother, the other if I did not marry her. So that I was certain of a hiding in any case from one or the other if the threats were carried out.

Then Anne Hartley and "Watercress Betty" had a stand-up fight outside our caravan to settle who had the best right to speak to me. This amused the neighbours, but greatly upset my father and mother, while I was unmercifully chaffed about it. At length, to avoid any further coil through my fatal attractions, father thought it best to leave the neighbourhood, and we moved to the yard of the "Three Mackerel," a public-house at a considerable distance from the "King Harry."

My parents didn't like leaving the old place, nor did I; but we could not hope for quiet if we remained. So off we went. Father grumbled, and had much to say about "his lordship's" conceit and vanity. Mother hoped it "would be a lesson to me"; and I felt that I was being unduly blamed.

Really, the fault was not mine if I was too good-looking for the ladies' peace of mind. That was my misfortune; one, by the way, that I have quite overcome now. At eighteen the girls all had their eyes on me. At eighty they turn their heads the other way. Heigh-ho! It is one of the reminders that I have had my day!

# CHAPTER XX

## I GO TO STEPNEY FAIR AND MEET MY FATE

STEPNEY FAIR, glorious old Stepney Fair, then the biggest gathering of the kind in England, was where I intended to make the first pitch with the new show. We worked hard to get everything complete, and on the Saturday before Easter Sunday, in the year of our Lord 1848, started from the "Three Mackerel" for Stepney Green so as to get a good pitch and have all in readiness for opening on Easter Monday, when the fair, which lasted three days, commenced.

Stepney was a very different place at that period to what it is today. Where now are thickly clustered houses and narrow streets was a vast open plain many acres in extent, part of it constituting Stepney Green. On this great space the fair was held.

To it from all quarters came showmen, cheapjacks, and dealers in wares of every possible kind and quality. It was also a great event with the London costermongers, who made lots of money by driving visitors in their carts and wagons at a half penny a head from Whitechapel Church to the Green, which is now only a name, but was then verdant, breezy grass-land, overlooked by the rambling, old fashioned Maid and Magpie Hotel.

Not far from the latter our new show was pitched, and there was no prouder showman in the great fair than myself as I came strutting out upon the platform in my Hamlet dress, while one of our men banged at a Chinese gong to attract the public.

My get-up was something quite fresh and novel, and I very soon had a big crowd round the front of the show, and I pattered to them in my best style. I defied all the wizards of the north, the east, and south, taking to myself the title of "Wizard of the West." At this time there were before the public many professors of magic, Anderson, Jacobs, Phillipy, Houdin, Kelly, Kenny, and Herr Dobler being all in the zenith of their fame. My only rival at the fair, however, was Na Barno Eagle, of whom I have previously spoken, and who was then making his last appearance with a travelling booth.

So I did very well indeed – much better, in fact, than I ever imagined I should do. My pretensions and my patter filled our show at every performance, and what is more, our patrons were well satisfied; for, I say it with all due modesty, I was really a skilled conjurer.

Not only the pleasure-seekers came to my entertainment, but numbers of the show-folk looked in to see the young pretender to professional fame in his Hamlet dress, and to give him a cheering word.

Amongst them was an exceedingly pretty girl – at least, I thought so – named Ellen Chapman, who was performing at Mr. George Wombwell's menagerie as Madame Pauline de Vere, the Lady of the Lions. She was one of the first women to thrill the public by entering a den of lions and tigers, and excited much wonder and admiration by the way in which she controlled the savage beasts, and made them obey her slightest commands.

We had known each other when quite children, for her father, like mine, travelled with a peepshow, and we had been much together in those early days of struggle and privation. I was delighted to renew the acquaintance, and to find, moreover, that she was equally pleased at our meeting. From that moment I knew that Nellie was the only girl in the world for me.

After the show we met and had a long talk, and my admiration became, if possible, stronger than ever, as she told me modestly enough of her triumphs she had been winning in her profession.

Mr. Wombwell had then just been with his menagerie before Queen Victoria, the Prince Consort and the Royal Household at Windsor Castle, for the especial purpose of giving Miss Chapman's exhibition.

Her late revered Majesty witnessed it from a window close to which the den was drawn up in the courtyard. At the conclusion Queen Victoria sent for Nellie and overwhelmed her with kindness and gracious praise.

When she entered the room in which the Royal pair were sitting, the Prince Consort patted her on the back, and the Queen, taking her by the hand, said, "Oh, my dear, are you not afraid? I do hope you will not get hurt. I felt so terrified when I saw you open the lion's mouth and put your head in its jaws. Dear, are you not afraid?"

"Oh no, your Majesty," was the faltering reply, for my dear girl said she felt more nervous in that room with Royalty, where all was kindness, than she ever had done in the lions' den.

The Queen then went to a large sideboard and from a casket took a beautiful gold watch and chain.

"Will you be kind enough to receive this and with it my best wishes for your safety?" asked her Majesty. Then, noticing that the girl, whose heart was full, was unable to reply, while tears of gratitude streamed down her cheeks, she again said, "I am sure you are afraid, Miss Chapman."

"No, your Majesty," Nellie then stammered out. "I am not afraid of the wild beasts, but I am nervous and overcome by kindness since I came into this room."

"Poor girl," said the Queen; "I hope and pray you will never get hurt. Good-bye and God bless you!"

While Stepney Fair lasted Nellie and I took every opportunity of meeting each other, and though I think Mr. Wombwell hardly liked my attention to his "star," whose presence in his menagerie after her performance before Queen Victoria was for the next three years worth, on his own admission, £100 a day to him, he saw no way to interfere. When, therefore, the time came for me to move on with my show, Nellie and I had reached a complete understanding, and had arranged to keep up a regular correspondence until the happy day should arrive for our union. Do you wonder that old Stepney Fair holds such high place in my memory and estimation?

# CHAPTER XXI

## HOW SHOWMEN TURNED FIREMEN

I HAVE reason to remember that particular Stepney Fair, quite apart from the fact that I left it an engaged man, by an exciting incident that occurred. There was an enormous rope factory on one side of the green, an establishment that extended over a piece of ground running quite into the country, and on the last day of the fair this was suddenly discovered to be on fire. It was just towards dusk when the flames were first seen, and in a very little time they had made tremendous headway.

The excitement was intense, the people flocking from the fair to witness the fire and to render what assistance they could. With the pleasure-seekers went the showmen, one and all, to give what aid was possible, and an extraordinary scene was the result.

There was no time to take off dresses, and amid the flying sparks, and in and about the burning buildings, could be seen clowns, knights in armour, Indian chiefs, jugglers in tights and spangles, rope-walkers in fleshings – in fact, all the characters of the fair in full dress, striving with might and main to combat the flames.

Here would be seen clown, pantaloon, harlequin, and demon passing buckets from hand to hand, while at another point was the feeble parish engine, manned by sweating Saracens, Crusaders, Roman gladiators, and such-like, pumping as though their very lives depended on their exertions. Up on the building, running along beams with crowbars and hatchets, were the tight-rope walkers, vaulters, and acrobats, whose training enabled them to go where no other persons could possibly have clambered, breaking away roofs and walls to prevent the spread of the fire. Over all was the glow of the flames lighting up the faces of the dense multitude that surged and swung and shouted its approval of the efforts of the motley-garbed show-folk to check the advance of the enemy.

It was a picture that would have delighted a painter of weird scenes, though he might have despaired of ever putting its wavering lights and shadows and the strange characters glancing through them effectively on canvas. I know it impressed itself indelibly on my memory, as in my Hamlet dress I took my share of work with the others in checking the roaring flames.

At last our efforts told, and we did check them, but not until enormous damage had been done. A big part of the works was, however, saved, and so pleased were the authorities at the spirit the showmen had exhibited that they gave orders for the fair to continue another day to help make up any losses we had sustained through leaving our booths to become fire-fighters.

We did rare business on that extra day, for the story of the fire had spread, and the public came in crowds to view the scene and to patronize the showmen who had worked so well.

# CHAPTER XXII

## THE SCHOOL FOR LEARNED PIGS

AT this period, besides the established fairs of London, such as Stepney, Wandsworth, Greenwich, and Deptford Trinity Monday Fair, where for many years the famous Duke of Wellington used to march in procession with the children, there had grown up a series of what were known as "New Fairs."

Three men, Fox, senior and junior, and George Young, who were connected indirectly with the show business, hit upon the idea as a speculation, and did remarkably well out of it. Wherever there was a large space of vacant land in any part of London – and there were plenty of such spaces in those days – this trio would, if possible, secure it for certain dates that they knew were not covered by regular fairs. Then they would call the travellers together and arrange for a fair for two, three, four, or six days, as the case might be, getting their profit out of the charges they made for each pitch.

The best and most successful of these new departures was King's Cross Fair. This was held on the very ground where the Great Northern Railway Station now stands. It was a vast piece of land utilized as a shooting-place for all the dust and rubbish of that part of London. When the time for the fair arrived the rubbish was hastily levelled down, and on it the shows and booths were pitched. It grew to be a really important gathering, and was held three times each summer for four days at a time. Shows of all sorts pitched at King's Cross Fair, more especially the smaller exhibitions, though I have on occasion seen the giants of the road, such as Wombwell's menagerie, in all their glory there, and doing very good business.

It was to King's Cross Fair that I moved from Stepney with my conjuring show, and very well I did with it, in spite of counter-attractions – and they were many – especially in the way of performing animals, such as fortune-telling ponies and "learned pigs".

The latter animals were just then very popular, the public being amazed at the idea that creatures generally considered so stupid should perform tricks such as picking out cards, that seemingly called for an exercise of unusual intelligence.

Well, all animals have intelligence of a kind, and, in regard to the "learned pig," I will explain how, by the craft of the showman, his small intelligence can be made to take on an air of real scholarship. "How simple!" you will say when you know how it's done. Quite so; but it is not everybody who knows how to utilize properly these simple things, otherwise the show business would be overcrowded.

Well, now, the making of a "learned pig" is upon this wise. You get your pig, fat and comfortable-looking and not too old, a fairly long stout stick, a leather strap that will buckle neatly round the pig's neck and has also a small plate and screw rivet that will attach it to the stick. Then you are ready to commence the lessons.

In the end of the stick, not the end to which the strap is attached, you bore a hole, and through this drive a long nail into the floor of your academy so that the stick can move freely round on it in a circle, but in no other way. When the pig's neck is buckled into the strap at the other end of the stick the animal is bound to move in a circle, of which the nailed end of the stick is the centre.

Then with a little cane to direct his movements you induce the pig to walk. Of course he goes round and round and round, for he can move in no other direction, and when he wants to stop, which is often, you just keep him going by gentle taps with the cane. When you have kept him walking round some time you begin to let him stop in his course now and again, but always just before the stop giving a slight click with the fingers. The slightest sound will do, merely the snap of the thumb-nail against the fingernail is sufficient. The pig will hear it, and in a very short time will stop anywhere in his monotonous walk directly he hears the slight signal.

You then vary the lesson by arranging a pack of cards face upwards just outside the circle, fixed, of course, by the length of the stick, which the pig traverses, and commence to patter as if to an audience somewhat in this style: "Well, Toby, you see the cards before you. Which is the ace of spades?" Any card you like you can, of course, name. Round goes the pig in his circle, and as he comes opposite the card "click" go your nails, and he at once stops.

"You see, ladies and gentlemen," you proceed, "Toby knows the cards. Will someone kindly name a card they would like him to pick out." Round goes piggy as you patter, and "click" you stop him where you like. In two or three days the pig, without the stick or the strap, will commence to move round at a tap from your switch whenever a circle of cards or persons is formed. He will also stop dead at the finger-click until the touch of the switch lets him know he must move on again. Then his education is complete.

You can send him round a circle of people, asking him to pick out the man that likes kissing the girls. In fact, vary your entertainment as you will, the pig will be listening for the "click," not to your patter, and will stop directly he hears it, while the audience will not notice the slight sound. With every performance the pig will improve, especially if you accustom him to receive after each show an apple, potato, or some such little luxury.

I have seen first-class learned pigs trained in a week by this simple method. Their intelligence consists almost entirely in having a sharp ear for the "click" that brings them a welcome stop in their walk. The rest of the performance that so amazes the onlookers is due to the showman's arrangement of his cards, his audience, and his patter.

In my long life I have found many wonderful things, besides the performance of the learned pig, whose entire art and mystery consists of a quick ear and a nimble tongue, and, incidentally, as you will discover if you follow my story, have profited thereby. We resolved, after leaving King's Cross, that we should do better in the country at the Statute fairs and wakes that we used to journey to with father and the peep-show than we should at the London new fairs. So we left them behind us and hopefully took to the open road.

When I say "we", I mean my brother John, myself, and John's wife, for John had got married some months before to a very nice young woman. She was a daughter of Sam Atkins, who, with Tom Atkins, started the Liverpool Zoological Gardens. This was the most important institution of its kind in the country at one period, and for some years made a lot of money.

Reverses, however, came upon the Atkins family, and they took to their old business of travelling the fairs again. Thus it was John met his wife. They were married from our winter pitch in the "King Harry" yard at old Whitechapel Church, since then burnt down, re-erected, and entirely altered.

I did not go to church to see the wedding, for all the others were anxious to be there, and as somebody had to stop behind to prepare the wedding feast, I volunteered for the purpose. What do you think the feast consisted of? Why nothing more nor less than plenty of beefsteaks and onions and potatoes. It was not a fashionable wedding banquet, but nevertheless a heartily enjoyed one. We had music with it, too, of a sort, for showmen friends and neighbours gathered round with pots, pans, and sticks, and made such a clatter that our ears sung with it. The "charivari," as it was called, was then the invariable accompaniment of a showman's wedding, and was done to bring luck to the newly married pair, at whose expense the bangers of the pots and pans were regaled with drinks. The noise gave me a headache, and I resolved that when it came to my turn to be noosed I would dodge the charivari, and I did, as you will discover.

# CHAPTER XXIII

## SECOND SIGHT AND A QUEER INCIDENT

MRS. JOHN SANGER was a very nice young woman, and a very clever one into the bargain. She soon learned to do a hanky-panky second-sight and thought-reading business with me that proved a capital draw, and always amazed our country patrons. The new business, which took the place of the *poses plastiques*, was productive of a very curious incident, whereby a little innocent jugglery on my part saved, I shall always maintain, a man's sanity, and possibly his life as well.

We had drifted in the course of our travels to Ashbourne, in the romantic and beautiful Dovedale district of Derbyshire, and at the August fair there did very well, the thought-reading and second-sight performance causing the greatest astonishment.

When our show was over somebody asked to see me, and I went out and found a very wild, worried-looking young farmer waiting for me. "Oh," he said, directly he caught sight of me, "do let me speak to you privately; I have something of the utmost importance to ask you."

"Very well," I said; "come in here," and took him into the living-wagon. "Now," I said, "what is it? What's the matter with you?"

"I have come to you," he said, "because I know you can help me, for I have seen your second-sight and know you are a true 'cunning-man.' Look at me. Do you think I am doomed to be hung?"

The startling question took me right aback, but I managed to keep my countenance and to ask him quietly, "Why do you imagine such a thing?" Then he told me he had had a terrible dream in which he thought he was being taken to the scaffold, and as he woke up struggling he thought he heard a voice say, "The gallows will be your end!"

He had, he said, dreamt the same dream three times running and could not rest for thinking of it. The poor fellow certainly looked very worn and haggard, and I resolved to see if I could ease his mind by a little pious deception. So I picked up a square of black velvet and said solemnly, "Give me your hand!" He did so. I placed the black velvet over it, then put my hand on top. "Now," I said, "shut your eyes and think of your dream."

He did as he was told, evidently fully believing I possessed occult powers. After keeping him a minute or two I said, "Open your eyes. Did you recall your dream?" "Yes," he said, with a shudder. "Well," I said, "while you were thinking of your dream I could see beyond it. It was nothing but a false vision of the scaffold, for I have seen that you will be happily married, have children, and die an old man in your bed!"

"Thank God!" said the poor fellow fervently.

"I knew you could tell me directly I saw your show. You have lifted a weight off my heart." Then he offered me some money, but my conscience wouldn't let me take it, and after thanking me again profusely; he went away with quite a cheerful look on his face.

Five years afterwards I was at a fair at Derby when a well-dressed man came up to me and said, "How do you do, Mr. Sanger? Do you remember me?" I said I did not recollect him, and he then told me that he was the young farmer who had asked my advice at Ashbourne over his strange dream. He had never worried any more about it after I had assured him it was a false vision; and fully believed I had saved him from madness or suicide.

He was happily married and had two children, whom he brought later on with his wife to see me. I was very glad my bit of hanky-panky turned out to be such a good thing in his case, and I felt that the little deception I had practised on him was more than justified by the result.

After Ashbourne we made our way out of the Derbyshire district in order to work back again towards London, taking the autumn fairs and race meetings as we went.

I had heard regularly from my sweetheart, who had left Wombwell's establishment and was travelling with her father, who had a large peep-show. They intended, she wrote, to winter in London, and that naturally determined me to do likewise.

# CHAPTER XXIV

## RACE GAMBLERS AND "TOG-TABLES"

So we travelled on, doing fairly good business, more especially at some of the race-meetings. At Lewes, I know, we did very well, for money was plentiful amongst the crowds there, and the "tog-tables" on the course did a roaring trade. These "tog-tables" were nothing more nor less than open-air gambling boards, for gambling at that time on race-courses was freely permitted. The tables were from twelve to fourteen feet long by about three feet wide, very handsomely constructed, and covered with painted cloths. For some feet round them were boards overlaid with nice thick carpets for the "flats" – I beg pardon, gamblers – to stand on.

Presiding over each table would be a handsome, luxuriously garbed woman possessed of a wonderful gift of patter. Most of these women were the wives or relatives of the table proprietors, who were, many of them, as wealthy as they were unscrupulous. The display of money made at these tables was marvellous, the silver being all newly-minted coin procured for the purpose. This silver, mostly crowns and half-crowns, was placed in a big network bag in full view of the people round the table. Nearby it was always a smaller bag of the same kind heavy with shining sovereigns.

When a sufficient crowd had gathered round the table the "tog-lady" would pick up the twelve large wooden dice with which the game was played, drop them into the big leather dice-box, and invite players to try their luck. To encourage the others one or two well-dressed fellows, who belonged to the table and acted as "bonnets," would call for a throw. The price of the latter was one shilling, or three might be had for half a crown. The prizes marked against certain of the numbers amongst the many painted-in squares on the cloth that covered the table varied from £1 to £100.

On a throw being called for the dice were rattled in the box by the "tog-lady," then suddenly thrown out with a circular sweep of the arm so as to spread them. Directly they were down she took a long stick with a great flat curved piece at the end like a reaper's sickle and drew the dice together into a square.

Then she would commence to count rapidly something like this: "Two and two are four, and one is five, and ten is fifteen, and five is twenty; a twenty one makes forty-one and three forty-four, and four forty-eight, and two is fifty, and eighteen makes sixty-eight, and six seventy-four, and seven eighty-one! Eighty-one is the number thrown! Let me see," and she would glance quickly over the painted squares. "Ah, eighty and eighty-two are prize winners. Eighty-one is a blank! Very near, indeed, sir, very near, indeed; try again; better luck next time!"

That, of course, would be an outsider's luck always. When a "bonnet" threw it would be: "Ah, your luck is in, sir! Number so-and-so wins ten golden sovereigns! There is your money, sir!" The coin would be counted out, and dozens of foolish onlookers, stimulated by the seeming good fortune of the "bonnets", would rush to put down their shillings, only to find that their "luck" was quite of another order.

As a variation, after drawing the dice together, the "tog-lady," with a quick glance at their tops – which she could see plainly, but those round could only glimpse at by craning their necks – would throw the curved stick across them, hiding many of the figures, and would say to the caller, "I'll give you five pounds for your throw, sir, before I count!"

Some of the "bonnets" would at once whisper to the caller, "Don't, don't you take it; she's twigged a big prize; make her count." In nine cases out of ten the advice would be taken. If by chance an outsider did take the "tog-lady's" offer, another bystander – of course a "bonnet" – would say that he had called for a throw first, that the offer and the money was his. A fierce wrangle would ensue, and the "tog-lady" would say, "I allow no quarrelling. The game is fair and square. If you are not satisfied I must throw again. Which of you takes the fresh throw?" The latter would be quickly made, with, of course, the usual result to the outsider.

So the game went merrily on with all the profits to the table, for I never heard of an outsider ever being allowed to make a win. But the crop of ninnies was a never-failing one, and the "tog-tables" always had a prosperous time. The proprietors made piles of money, yet I cannot remember that any of them greatly benefited by their ill-gotten gains in the end. One of the most famous "tog-table" owners and gamblers was John James, reputed at one period to be worth £100,000. When the race-course gambling was stopped he took a large hotel at Stepney. A fire and some unlucky racing and company speculations, however, brought him to complete ruin, and he died in the workhouse, as many of his class had done before him.

# CHAPTER XXV

## MORE JUSTICES' JUSTICE

WHILE we were travelling towards London, father, who, accompanied by William and my mother, was also moving in that direction, though on another route, had been having a little adventure with his peep-show.

This was at Warminster, a small but very ancient town lying to the south-west of Salisbury Plain, whither he had gone, as usual, for the big autumn fair. The old custom had always been for the showmen to draw into the town to take up their pitches the day before the fair. But authorities had come into power who did not recognize old customs, and who, moreover, desired, as one of them said, "to keep the vagabond showmen in their place."

The Mayor of Warminster, who was a man of very narrow opinions, looked upon show-people as little better than emissaries of the Evil One, and resolved to harass them accordingly. He had been told by his clerk, or some other wiseacre, that if the showmen drew into the town the night before the fair and slept in their caravans, as the latter were in no sense houses, they could be arrested for the atrocious crime of "sleeping out," and so dealt with as "rogues and vagabonds."

My father on this particular night had, therefore, no sooner got warm in bed in his caravan, which lay on the outskirts of the fair, than down came the beadle of the parish with his three-cornered hat and gilt staff and two assistants and arrested him. They also from an adjoining caravan took Richard Hunter, who had a travelling museum, and then conveyed their two protesting prisoners to the lock-up.

The next morning they were brought before the Bench and duly charged with sleeping out as against the "statute made and provided." The mayor, who presided, read them a long lecture on the iniquity of their calling, and said that in order to show the other caravan-dwellers the pains and penalties their "irregular" mode of life rendered them liable to he had resolved to treat the prisoners as "rogues and vagabonds," and they would be sentenced to twenty-one days' hard labour each.

Here was an example of justices' justice with a vengeance, but my brave old dad was equal to the occasion.

"Stop a minute, your worship," he said, "Stop a minute! You have no power to send us to prison, for we were not trespassing and were sleeping under a roof. In my case, too, I carry the Royal Prescription allowing me to get my living as I choose, providing I do it honestly. I'm only a poor showman, but I know the law, and you will have to pay for this outrage."

One or two of the other justices looked rather uncomfortable at this, but the mayor said, "Pooh! What is your word worth? What's this nonsense about a Royal Prescription, eh?"

At this my father pulled out a little waterproof bag which he always carried hung round his neck by a cord, and, opening it, took out a parchment.

"Here," said he, "is the document. I served his late Majesty King George for ten long years as a sailor, and was with Nelson on the *Victory* at Trafalgar. When I left, I got ten pounds a year pension and this parchment, which, amongst other things, says: 'James Sanger, as aforesaid, having so done service for his Majesty in the wars with France, is hereby privileged and entitled to carry on any trade, craft, or profession whereby he may honestly provide for himself, in any manner he may consider suitable to the needs of the said trade, craft, or profession.'" The document further went on to give the holder certain exemptions and travelling rights, and to declare that those interfering with those rights might incur certain penalties. After it had been handed to the justices and perused by them, it was given back to my father, and the mayor said: "I have never before seen such a document. I cannot say whether it is yours or not, but I will give you the benefit of the doubt. You ought to go to gaol, both of you, but this time you may go away."

So father, and Hunter with him, both went free, and did very well at the fair, in spite of the mayor's attempt to interfere with them. They afterwards consulted a lawyer to see if they could get any compensation for their arrest, but the man of law advised them to let well alone, as it would cost a lot of money to bring an action, the result of which, even if they gained it, would hardly be likely to pay them for their trouble.

We heard the story when we got to London and forgathered for the winter, and it made us very angry. Father wanted the showmen to join together for mutual protection, and one or two informal meetings were held with a view to forming a society. The meetings, however, had no practical result, though there was much talk at them, father being particularly strong in his denunciation of the country authorities. Ah, we little thought as we heard the hale old man so roughly eloquent how soon we were to lose him!

# CHAPTER XXVI

## HOW THE MUMMERS GAINED A VICTORY

THE spring of 1849 was a brilliant one, and we started on the road after our wintering full of spirits. I had arranged to get married to Nellie Chapman as soon as I could command a certain sum of money, and that I hoped to get together before twelve months were over.

Man, however, proposes, but God disposes, and the truth of that saying was to be borne in upon me in a remarkable way in that memorable year.

We did fairly well on the road as we went along, taking always sufficient for current expenses, but never enough to allow a very big margin for saving. At last we reached Coventry in time for the May Fair, which, though not the principal one of the ribbon town, was always very good for business.

The fair was held on a sort of triangular green, a fine open space near the head of the town, and there was a large muster of showmen, Wombwell's, amongst others, making their way like ourselves to Lichfield and Walsall for the great Whitsuntide fairs at those two places.

I mention Wombwell's show in particular because two incidents occurred in connection with it that season that will never be effaced from my memory.

We came into Coventry on the Saturday, the fair being fixed for Monday, and took up our ground on the allotted space as quickly as possible. Wombwell's, as usual, got the best pitch, to which, indeed, they considered themselves entitled, pushing out of the way some wagons belonging to a very superior theatrical company at that time on the road.

This company belonged to Latimer, Loon and James, all well-known actors. The proceedings of Wombwell's men were very much resented by them, and rather high words arose, ending with a threat on the part of the actors that one day when the menagerie people wanted to take a similar liberty with regard to the ground they would give them a surprise.

They kept their word, as I shall show you, but for the time matters quieted down, and that Saturday night everything was got in readiness for the fair, all of us rejoicing in the prospect of a comfortable Sunday's rest prior to commencing business.

In the morning, after a good bath, I took a stroll round the fair ground, visiting amongst other shows the big menagerie. Here in the centre of the great space made by the drawn-up beast wagons was a big fire in an iron basket, and on it a pot containing the greens for the Sunday dinner, my old friend Bill Wombwell being busily engaged in looking to the welfare of the boiling.

Bill, who was as good a fellow as ever breathed, was a nephew of old George Wombwell, and acted as head keeper to the menagerie. As I came up to him he said, "Hullo, George, how goes it?" "Pretty well!" I answered. "But what's the matter, Bill? You look very solemn."

"I'm hanged if I know," was his reply, "but I've had a feeling ever since I got up this morning that something's wrong, that something's going to happen to me. I was just thinking as you came in that I was cooking the greens but shouldn't be able to eat 'em."

"Don't be a fool, Bill," I said to him. "You have got an attack of liver, that's all." "Perhaps that is it," he replied, and then we fell to talking of other things. While we were in conversation there was a sound of restlessness amongst the animals at the farther end of the menagerie. "It's the elephants," said Bill, in answer to my glance. "Somebody has upset big Jimmy in some way, and he's as fidgety as he can be. I'll go down and have a look at him before I have my dinner."

We talked a little longer, and then I went off to our caravan for the Sunday's meal. We had hardly sat down to it when we heard a noise outside of people talking excitedly and moving past in a crowd. "What's up?" said my brother John; and his wife, who had gone outside for a moment, answered the question as she came in, white as a ghost, by saying, "Good God! Poor Bill Wombwell's killed!"

The news stunned me. I could hardly believe that the healthy, strong man I had left not many minutes previously was dead. But so it was. He had gone to see the elephants, as he said he should, and directly he entered their den "Big Jimmy" had knocked him down and crushed the life out of him. The elephant had been teased or ill-used by somebody, had worked himself up into a rage, and poor Bill Wombwell was the victim.

I could not help thinking of Bill's premonition. It might have been nothing more than coincidence, but it was very strange all the same, and impressed me strongly at the time. I know it spoiled Coventry May Fair for me, and I was very glad when we moved on to Lichfield.

At the latter place nothing particular happened, and we moved out on the night of Whit-Monday for Walsall, ten miles from Lichfield, for the big Whit-Tuesday fair held in the Market Place. There was always a rush for the ground here, and Latimer, Loon and James, with their big theatre, got on the very spot Wombwell's fancied.

Accordingly Wombwell's men drove their heavy wagons into the theatre vans, which were full of valuable scenery and properties, in a most disgraceful manner. Then suddenly a diversion occurred. The actors, evidently prepared, swarmed out, each with a pickaxe, crowbar, or similar heavy weapon, and attacked the backs of the beast wagons that were being forced against the lighter theatre vans.

"We're ready for you!" was their cry. "You can take our place and smash our property, but we'll let your beasts loose!" They meant what they said, too, as they bashed at the panels of the dens containing the wild animals, who would very soon have been out in the fair, with God only knows what consequences.

I know the thought of it frightened me, and it scared Wombwell's men as they never were scared before. Almost without a word the big beast wagons were quickly drawn away from those belonging to the theatre and put in position elsewhere. The actors were left in possession of the ground they had been first to take, and we all rejoiced at their victory, for Wombwell's Menagerie, by virtue of its size and importance, had long considered itself king of the road, for whom all others must make way at command. More than one showman took a drink in Walsall that day to the toast, "Bravo, the Mummers."

After leaving Walsall, we visited various small places, and as we travelled we heard that cholera was raging throughout the country. At last we came across a notification by the Board of Health concerning the disease, and learned from it that since March cholera had broken out in twelve different parts of the Metropolis and that twenty-seven towns in England and Wales and seventeen towns in Scotland were affected.

This damped our spirits considerably, for so great was the dread of cholera that the attendance at fairs and wakes was bound to be considerably affected, with consequent loss to ourselves. It was even as we feared. Business grew worse and worse, and in September, when the deaths from cholera in London had mounted up to over three thousand weekly, we hardly took enough money to keep ourselves going.

In the circumstances we considered that it would be useless for us to attempt to get back to London for the winter, and resolved to make the best of it during the non-travelling months in Liverpool. Bad was the best, and how we worried through I don't know. But worry through we did, and with the spring were on the road again, very hard up, but hoping to make a bit at the northern spring fairs to give us a start in the year that was to be one, though we knew it not then, of strangely mixed joy and sorrow for us.

# CHAPTER XXVII

## I LOSE MY FATHER AND GAIN A WIFE

IN the very first month of 1850 we got some bad news. This was to the effect that my sweetheart's cousin, Miss Bright, who had taken her place with Mr. Wombwell as Lion Queen, had been killed by a tiger. The sad affair took place at Chatham on January 11th, the beast so mauling the poor girl that she died only a few moments after being taken from the den.

The tiger was one with which my sweetheart had frequently performed, and when I heard the terrible news I felt thankful that Nellie had abandoned the Lion Queen business. At the same time I must say I do not think she would have had any trouble with the tiger, her method being very different to that adopted by Miss Bright. The latter had been begged by Nellie again and again not to irritate the animals by tapping at them with a riding-whip, which she was very fond of doing, as she thought it made them smart in their movements. There was no necessity for this flicking at them; all that was needed was to move the whip left or right, as the case might be, and the animals would follow it. But Miss Bright preferred to give them sharp little stinging cuts, with the result that the tiger became angry and made her his victim.

I may as well say here that I have never known a wild beast kill a keeper or trainer unless the animal had been previously ill-used or tormented. In poor Bill Wombwell's case it was afterwards shown that the elephant had been goaded and upset by an under-keeper. In Miss Bright's case she had flicked her whip about the tiger's eyes. At the Crystal Palace, when my elephant Charlie killed a man, it was made abundantly clear that the fellow had brought his fate on himself by persistent cruelty. It is as well that the public should understand these things, and should know that there is no danger to any performer with wild beasts so long as the animals have not been unduly irritated by some act of unkindness.

But I must get on with my story, the next scene of which lies at Stalybridge Wakes, where we found ourselves nearly penniless. The wakes were very rough affairs in those days, the Lancashire lads and lasses making holiday at them in the wildest possible fashion. Rows were frequent, and now and again terrible scenes were enacted, men and women being literally kicked to fragments by the formidable iron-tipped, clogs which formed the general footwear. Lancashire men in those days gave very little attention to the use of their fists. The clog was their weapon, and they considered there was nothing unmanly in kicking and biting to death – for they would use their teeth like dogs – any person who had the misfortune to incur their anger.

There was a callous brutality about a Lancashire mob in those days that, looking back, now strikes one as simply appalling. At the very wakes of which I am now speaking we were afforded a shocking example of it.

Nearly opposite our show was a large ginger-bread stall kept by a man whose name I am almost sure was Sheppard, a big, good-humoured fellow; and a well-known fair-goer. I was on the platform with John outside our show just getting ready to call the people up when we noticed a row at Sheppard's gingerbread stall.

He seemed to be expostulating with a crowd of miners about something, when all at once over went his stall, and the next minute he himself was under their feet with all of them kicking at him anywhere and everywhere as hard as they could. From our position on the platform we could see the poor fellow's body with the heavy clogs battered into it as though it was a stuffed sack instead of a human thing.

I wanted to go down to interfere, but John held me back, saying, "It's no use, boy! They'd only serve you the same!" And so they would have done, I have no doubt. At any rate, though the crowd formed a sort of ring, nobody stirred a hand to save the man who was being kicked to pulp in the centre of it.

"Kicked to pulp" is by no means too strong an expression, for that is what literally happened to the poor ginger-bread seller. When the crowd with the kickers suddenly melted away there lay the body – I can see it now – a ghastly, shapeless thing in the clear sunlight, with the white dust of the roadway blotched here and there about it with purple stains. It was one of those things that a man once seeing carries for ever after as a shuddering recollection, and I never hear the name Stalybridge but the picture of that battered, awful object lying prone in the sunlight comes before me.

Some little time after the brutal deed had been done one or two constables made a leisurely appearance, looked at the body as though such sights were common to their ordinary day's work, and the corpse was removed. I never learned what verdict the coroner's jury returned concerning Sheppard's death, or whether any attempt was ever made to bring any of his assailants to justice. I had trouble of my own at hand that was to completely engross my attention. That very night we received the heart-breaking news that our dear father was dead. We could scarcely believe it, for when we had last seen him he looked very hale and hearty, and as if he had many years before him.

My brave, splendid, kindly, resourceful father, who had brought his children up in a way that earned their fondest love and respect and made useful men and women of them, had, it appears, fallen a victim to the cholera.

After rising to an appalling height in September, the disease suddenly checked its course, and at the end of October, 1849, London was officially declared to be free of it. In the spring, however, it showed a very slight recrudescence, and at Rotherhithe claimed two victims, my father, who had his peep-show at St. Helena's Gardens there, being one of them. The other was also a showman, who was seized with the disease at the same time as my father.

Our grief was bitter, and it was added to by the fact that William's letter, which brought the news of father's death, intimated that things had not been going well with the show, and that mother would either have to sell or pawn something to provide a proper funeral, or go in debt for it. We also had been doing badly, and we, too, must sell or pawn something if we wanted to get to town in time for the burial. But, talking it over between us, we decided that the latter would be sure to be hurried in a case of cholera, and that if we packed up at once we should never reach London in time for it. Moreover, if mother was in want of money it was our duty to stay out the fair on the chance of getting some to send to her. We knew father would have wished this, and we decided that it was our best course.

So we stayed through the wake with smiles and merry words for our patrons, who little knew the sorrow in our hearts as we jested, and, working our hardest, drew big audiences. When we had finished we found we had twelve pounds to send to mother, and that gave us some little satisfaction and assuagement in our trouble.

After Stalybridge things brightened with us. We did well at nearly every place we visited, and when we got to Sheffield for the

November Fair, there was enough money in hand to enable me to compass the dearest wish of my life – namely, my union with Nellie Chapman.

Nellie was at Sheffield with her father's peep-show, for it had been arranged that we should meet there, and on the Sunday following the fair, which lasted a week, we were married amid the good wishes of our friends at Sheffield's ancient parish church of St. Peter.

As I told you, I had resolved to avoid the usual charivari if possible; so soon after the ceremony was over we took train – our first railway ride, by the way – to London. With us on a special truck came my show, for I was resolved to try my luck once more in the great Metropolis.

# CHAPTER XXVIII

## THE PANTOMIME PLAYED IN A CHARNEL HOUSE

I NOW come to one of the most curious incidents in my career, one that in the present state of society would be impossible, but that in the days of which I am writing was thought little or nothing of. Anxious to make a London reputation, I resolved, after consultation with John, to run a sort of winter theatrical show in conjunction with the conjuring.

So we took a large building in Clement's Lane, Strand, a thoroughfare that ran through to Clare Market, but has now been destroyed, the Law Courts standing on a portion of it.

This building, though very convenient for our purpose at the time, was one with a most unsavoury reputation. It was none other than the notorious Enon Chapel, erected as a speculation by a Nonconformist minister, who trusted to make it a paying one by taking advantage of the lax and insanitary conditions under which the dead were allowed to be disposed of prior to the passing of the Burial Act of 1850.

According to the facts given before the Committee of the House of Commons which was appointed to inquire into the system of London interments  facts that I may say I only learned later – Enon Chapel was registered for burials in 1823. From that date until the beginning of 1842, when the minister died, and the chapel after his interment in it was closed as a place of worship, over twelve thousand bodies were buried in the lower part of the chapel, only separated from the upper portion by a boarded floor. This space, in which the interments took place, was 60 feet by 30 feet and 6½ feet deep. Think of it, you who are blessed by the splendid sanitary arrangements of this age, and imagine what it meant in a crowded neighbourhood then, if you can!

Well, a few months after the chapel was closed it fell into the hands of other speculators. These worthies put a single brick floor over the old wooden one, another wooden one on the top of the bricks, and then proceeded to make money by turning this charnel house into a low dancing-saloon.

There was no secret about the dancing being over the dead. That, in fact, was made one of the attractions, for an old bill, which well shows the character of the place and the kind of persons who used it, ran as follows:-

Enon Chapel. – Dancing on the Dead. – Admission Three pence. No lady or gentleman admitted unless wearing shoes and stockings.

The scenes at Enon Chapel inspired some of Cruikshank's most biting caricatures, and at length, in 1848, a well-known surgeon of the day, a Mr. George Walker, purchased the place, in order to put an end to the scandal. At his own expense Mr. Walker entered into a contract with a builder to have all the bodies removed to Norwood Cemetery, and the floor properly bricked and cemented over. The cost was very great, for the men engaged in the gruesome work, which was done at night, had to be paid enormous wages; but the public-spirited surgeon saw the work through, and then allowed the place to pass out of his hands again.

It had been empty some months when I took it, in December, 1850, and I at once fitted it up as a theatre, with proscenium, stage-front, wings, and scenery, and, after trying the conjuring once or twice, opened it as a penny gaff pure and simple.

We engaged, amongst others, James Crockett, who was afterwards noted as a lion-tamer; Dan Harvey, of Connoly and Harvey, a very popular actor; Simpson, another good actor, and the first man who introduced the seizing bears and dogs in mock combat; Watty Hilyard, the celebrated clown, who afterwards played at Covent Garden and all the large, provincial theatres.

We played a round of pieces, gaff fashion, and for Christmas put on the pantomime, "The Ice Witch, or Frozen Hard; or, Harlequin and the Mountain of Snow." Being a fairly good operatic dancer, I played "Patchy," alias Harlequin, and Mrs. George Sanger skipped it on the light fantastic toe as Columbine. We gave five performances on Boxing Day, and engaged a band of twelve performers, who, in a wagonette drawn by two horses, used to play up and down the Strand and in other streets in the neighbourhood to advertise this unlicensed place of amusement.

Business was excellent, and we seemed likely to make a lot of money, when a sudden stop was put to our show. A police inspector who was an intimate friend of mine gave me a call and told me that it had been discovered that the contract or engaged by Mr. Walker had not fully carried out the terms made as to the removal of the bodies from Enon Chapel.

Some of his men had made known the fact that, over a hundred barrels of human bones and remains, and, as a sort of grim joke, the coffin of the minister himself, instead of being removed, had been cemented up in the floor at one end of the building – in fact, under the very spot over which my stage was erected. The authorities, who were not favourably disposed towards gaffs, had resolved, as they were empowered to do under the new Burial Act, to raid and close the building until the remains were properly disposed of.

But the hint was sufficient for me without troubling the authorities. I was horrified to think that our pantomime had been carried on over the dead. I had heard much by this time of the awful history of the building, and resolved to clear out right away. So we stopped all the performances forthwith, dismissed our band, and removed all our properties and scenery to some large sheds in the Mile End Road. Here in a big room we arranged a masquerade ball to dance the old year out and the new year in. But we did not get much by this, for in the small hours of the morning the dancing brought down the ceiling of a bar under the ballroom, smashed jugs, bottles, and glasses, put an end to the festivities, and brought us in a heavy bill for damages.

With the coming of the New Year we expected to do great things, for it was the year of happy augury, that of the International Exhibition of 1851. Much was looked for from this exhibition, the first of its kind, but I do not think it is any treason to say now that greatly as it was lauded at the time, and for long afterwards, possibly because of the many exalted personages connected with it, in its results it was really very disappointing.

One thing, however, it certainly did do. It helped to mark the immense improvement that had taken place since the accession of Queen Victoria in the condition of the English nation and the people. It crystallized, as it were, these improvements under one vast roof for all to see; it brought home to the people the fact that they were living in times infinitely better than they could have imagined possible but a few short years before, and encouraged them to look and work for still better times to come. For this, even if it did nothing more, the exhibition amply justified those who called it into being.

Times were indeed better. As compared with the days of my boyhood it was almost as though a miracle had been wrought in the land. The giant of steam was responsible for much of the transformation. Railways were stretching over the country, rendering a transport and interchange of commodities possible with a quickness and at prices that the old folks could never have dreamt of. Gas was becoming quite a common illuminant, while we had lamps and oils that made the rushlight and tallow flare period very dim indeed by comparison.

# CHAPTER XXIX

## A DISAPPOINTING FAIR AND AN EXPLOSION

TALKING of illuminants reminds me that we had made a big stride with them in the show business. We had achieved the naphtha lamp. I was the first to bring the new light to London. We found it at Huddersfield, the invention of a journeyman metalworker, and it made a wonderful sensation in the Mile End Road. With our naphtha lamps flaring brightly we would walk up and down, a crowd pressing at our heels to follow us eventually to the show, for which the new lights proved one of the best advertisements we had ever invested in.

Like most other show-folk of the day, we intended to take advantage of the Exhibition Fair, which was to commence on 1st May and continue while the International show in Hyde Park was open. Looking at the number of visitors the exhibition was bound to attract to London, we all anticipated that we should make money, and prepared accordingly.

The fair was held on a great piece of waste ground at Knightsbridge that was waiting for the builder, and a brave display the multitude of shows and caravans made when they had taken up their various pitches and were duly arranged in order. Everything seemed to promise well till the opening day. Then our spirits sank to zero, for it rained in torrents. Bad weather was the one thing we feared to mar our prospects, but we never anticipated it could be half as bad as it turned out to be on this occasion.

There was very little business done on the first day of the fair, and the second proved worse still, for it rained harder than ever. When the deluge continued on the third and fourth days our faces grew very long indeed. It was useless opening the shows, for nobody came to see them in the pouring rain, and we seemed bound to be ruined. Two days' fine weather gave us some heart again, for visitors were plentiful, though the fairground was like a quagmire. But our hopes were soon dashed, for after the two days' respite down came the rain again harder than ever.

It was a terrible time. The rain poured down every day, and the rough ground on which the fair was pitched grew into a great slough, the caravans sinking over the hubs of the wheels into the mud. The shows made a pitiful sight, the once gay fronts of the big travelling theatres, of which there were an unusual number at this fair, being turned into drooping, soddened masses of canvas, whose painted devices had dissolved into a streaky, many-coloured blur.

Their losses must have been immense, for they were the chief travelling establishments of their day, costing an enormous sum of money to keep going. For instance, amongst other theatres there were those of Wylde, Thorne, Smith, and Webster (two actors of the same names as the then proprietors of the Haymarket), and Patch and Bennett. The latter partners had one of the biggest theatres on the road, as well as several regular local concerns. Mr. Bennett, who now owns the theatre at Leicester, is the grandson of the Bennett of my day.

At last things got so bad that it was determined that the fair should be abandoned. How to get the caravans off the ground was the question, for they had sunk so deep in mud that the horses could not move them. Eventually some two hundred men were engaged by the showmen generally to do what the horses could not do. In batches of fifty, sixty, and even a hundred, they tailed on to stout ropes fastened to the various vehicles, and so drew them one by one to the main road.

The only showman who made any money out of that disastrous London season was Mr. William Batty, the then proprietor of Astley's. He built a large hippodrome close to Messrs. Tattersall's establishment, made it bright, comfortable, and weatherproof, and did well. His partner in the venture was a Mr. Bullard, who later became the founder of a well-known brewing firm.

Sick with disappointment over the collapse of the fair, from which we had expected so much, we took to the road again, and, the weather improving, did enough business to keep us going comfortably and to enable us to winter without hardship in Liverpool. From that port we set out again in the spring on what I called our northern circuit, and did very well through the spring and summer, the beginning of the autumn finding us in Sheffield.

On September 14th that year – 1852 – the great Duke of Wellington died, and the magnificence of his obsequies was the talk of the land. I saw an opportunity in it for an exhibition that might prove very attractive in the winter months, during which I was now keeping out of London. So I arranged with a noted Sheffield firm of magic-lantern makers for two big lanterns and sixteen scenes of the duke's funeral procession, painted on glass, each plate being fifteen inches by four inches in size. These each threw a good picture upon a white sheet some twenty feet square, and worked, one after the other slowly, had the effect of a large panorama. In addition to the funeral, I had forty other slides, representing the search of Sir James Ross in the Arctic regions for Sir John Franklin. It was a subject much in favour with the people of that time, and with the story which I had off by heart and told as the pictures were displayed the entertainment was really a very attractive one.

The oxy-hydrogen or limelight for lantern purposes had then been introduced, so I had my lanterns fitted with the necessary apparatus, and soon learned how to make the oxygen gas from a mixture of perchlorate of potash and other things that any local chemist could supply. The hydrogen was, of course, obtained from the ordinary gas of commerce. When my preparations were complete I took various halls and rooms in the large towns of the Midlands for a winter tour.

It was not, however, to pass without a disaster. One night we were engaged in making the oxygen gas in the caravan in which we lived ready for an exhibition at the Town Hall, Northwich. The retort was upon the fire whilst I was busy with the curling-tongs to give my hair a graceful wave, and the grease-paint to put the necessary archness and colour into my face. Mrs. Sanger was also getting into her finery in order to be ready to assist in working the show, and all seemed well.

Suddenly there was a tremendous report, a blinding flash of light all around us, and the walls of the carriage which was our home flew all to pieces. The retort had exploded.

When we recovered from the shock we found that our injuries were very serious. My wife, who had been blown clean out of the end of the caravan, was badly bruised, her hair singed off, and her face and arms much burned. My beautifully curled locks had disappeared with my light moustache and chin-piece, my dress-coat had fallen off me in tinder, while my hands and face were scorched to blackness. All that was left of the caravan was the floor and undercarriage. The rest was smithereens!

The report of the explosion had been heard, it was said, a mile away, and a crowd soon collected about our ruined home. Three doctors turned up, and two of them remained all night to look after us, applying any amount of lint and liniment to our smarting bodies, and giving us doses of laudanum at intervals. When morning broke we found, to add to our troubles, that we had been robbed. Some scoundrels had taken advantage of our injuries to steal all that was left worth stealing of our home. Worst of all they had taken the tin box that held our savings, and all the money left to us was a few shillings I happened to have in my pocket when the explosion took place.

# CHAPTER XXX

## MY FIRST CHILD IS BORN AND I LOSE MY MOTHER

IT was an awful predicament, but I managed to keep a stiff upper lip all the same. The authorities were very kind to us. They had found that the explosion was caused through a mistake on the part of the chemist's assistant, who had made up our gas-producing mixture, and they suggested that I should receive some charitable contributions. But these I steadfastly refused. As I told the mayor, who came to see me three times, my father had always said, "Never eat the bread of charity if you can avoid it," and, remembering his words, I intended to be very hungry indeed before I accepted a meal.

My attitude did me no harm. I was kept in Northwich nine days waiting for what repairs could be done to the old carriage, and as my right hand had escaped injury, though my left was burned, I announced a miscellaneous entertainment. This was held for two nights, and I did some conjuring while my wife took on the second-sight business. Prices were low, for Northwich was not a rich town, and the room when full only held about twelve pounds. But we filled it to the uttermost each night, and as I patted the good money in my pockets I said to myself, "On your legs again, George – on your legs, again!"

Meanwhile, the local joiners had been doing what they could to patch up our old caravan, and had made the best job they could of it. It again bore something of its original semblance, and with plenty of paint and putty looked quite bright.

Looks, however, were its chief qualifications, as we soon discovered when we started on the road in it again. When it began to rain the water made its way through the roof as through a sieve. The sides opened and the wind whistled in through innumerable cracks, so that we were very little better off than if we had been in the open air, and as it was a bitter winter, with plenty of frost and snow, our situation was not one to be envied.

I was the more concerned as Mrs. Sanger was in a delicate condition, and was very glad when at last I found her comfortable lodgings in Derby, whence I went forth to earn what I could in the places round about.

One of these places was Alton Towers, a little town, or, rather, a large village, where I took a big room up an hotel yard. Then I put on my Hamlet costume and strutted round the adjacent villages announcing at the top of my voice the wonderful show that was to be seen that night in Alton Towers. I got a good audience, and amongst them a doctor's son and a farmer's son, who were on the eve of going to America to seek their fortunes. They were very much interested in the sleight-of-hand business, and I arranged to give them lessons and to provide them with certain apparatus for ten pounds.

This I did, and I have reason to believe that on the other side of the water these enterprising young men quickly pushed their little knowledge of conjuring into a big business. In fact, I am certain they did, for I have known many people who met them in the States, and I have received letters and posters from them,

I intended to do three shows at Alton Towers; but was very anxious to see my wife, for a young Sanger had come to town, and she was sixteen miles away, in Derby. I knew she had no money, and was very desirous of giving her some, as well as of getting a sight of the new-comer. There was no railway there, or other means of conveyance, but I took courage in both hands, and walked to Derby. Then, when I had seen my wife and little one, I walked back, doing the whole thirty-two miles in time to repeat my exhibition at Alton. I had an excellent audience, to whom I showed my views of the Duke of Wellington's funeral and the Arctic exploration, and though no gas was available, and the lanterns were lit with seal oil and cotton wicks, everything was declared to be most satisfactory.

As my wife became convalescent I made arrangements for a little tour in Scotland, thinking that my miscellaneous show of panorama and conjuring would prove a paying novelty in that country. But I had reckoned without Scotch superstition and narrow religious prejudices. I quickly found that conjuring was looked upon as a very wicked business indeed, and people standing in front of my show would denounce it as the work of the devil.

To such lengths eventually did this open hostility proceed that upon Saturdays we were not allowed to perform at all because the day was too near to the Sabbath. In some villages we were informed that the minister had heard of our coming and had made special prayer in the kirk that rain might spoil our show if we ventured to open it.

I have done well in Scotland since then; in fact, have seen some of my most prosperous times there, and have made some of my best and dearest friends amongst its people. But that first reception made me very sick at the time of the "land o' cakes," and I turned back and made my way out of the bonnie country as speedily as I could.

Soon after leaving Scotland we suffered another terrible bereavement in the death of my dear old mother. She had joined us at Newcastle, whither she had journeyed specially from London in order to spend a little time with us and to make the acquaintance of her new grandson.

We had been in North Shields for the fair which is held on the first Friday in November, and had done fairly well, mother, who seemed in the best of health and spirits, quite enjoying her return to the old show life. On leaving Shields we were making our way to Darlington for the big mid-November fair there, and just as we were nearing Houghton-le-Spring, in Durham, mother was taken suddenly ill, and died within an hour of the doctor being fetched to her.

I shall never forget in that time of misery the kindness we received at the hands of the good people of Houghton-le-Spring. The colliers and their wives (for Houghton is the centre of a mining district) showed us a tender sympathy that could not have been greater had we been relatives and close friends instead of travelling strangers. When the dear old lady was laid to rest in the beautiful little churchyard of St. Michael, which lies in the very centre of the village, they all turned out for the funeral, most of them bringing bunches of evergreens to strew on the grave as a tribute of respect. Their attitude touched me deeply. It was one of those spontaneous outpourings that now and again occur to remind us that men and women, however much divided by blood and race, are, after all, one kin, one family, and it has helped to make that sad occasion one of my sweetest memories.

But, having buried our beloved dead, the necessities of life pressed themselves once more upon us; we were bound to be up and doing if we were to live. So, leaving with a local mason money to erect a stone to mother's memory, directly the solemn ceremony was over we had perforce to put our horses in the caravans, of which we had two, and press on for Darlington, for we had been in Houghton-le-Spring four days.

It was on a Sunday that we started, and oh, what a journey that was! We had not been long on the road when there came on a dreadful thunderstorm which lasted for hours, the rain pouring in torrents. The roads were little better than a succession of steep hills; indeed, it is not exaggerating to call them mountains, and in many cases it was necessary to push the carriages in order to enable the horses to climb the precipitous highways. So we got drenched through and through, and when we got into Darlington at five in the morning were completely beaten. Our staff of five did the best they could in their wretched condition, and my wife with our little baby and myself lay down to snatch a few hours' rest on the bed on which my mother but a few days previously had breathed her last.

That was an awful time, and we were frightfully depressed, for we had had about a month previously two deaths in our small company, one of them being that of the wife of Watty Hilyard, the clown. It was quite a relief, therefore, when daylight came to bustle about and build up the show. It was all ready about ten o'clock, and as I donned my Hamlet dress and strutted out, hiding an aching heart under my professional smile, I was cheered to see a waiting crowd ready with its pennies to witness the performance. We wanted those pennies badly, for we had run out of food and looked to our patrons to supply us with the wherewithal for a midday meal.

# CHAPTER XXXI

## I MEET YORK'S LORD MAYOR AND MANY MISFORTUNES

WE did very well at Darlington, and from there went on to York for the great hiring fair. Here we got an unpleasant surprise. No sooner did the authorities hear that ours was a conjuring show than they served us with a notice to quit the town within an hour on the ground that we were "rogues, vagabonds, and deceivers of the people."

Here was a pretty predicament. York, great city as it was, was years behind its smaller neighbours in the matter of freedom in regard to laws and regulations, and still wore the trammels of the dark ages. I was in despair, and as I pulled down my show, exclaiming bitterly against the treatment I was receiving, a gentleman came up. He was quite a stranger to me, but at once told me that he had heard what had happened, and invited me to come down to Peasenholme, where the city authorities had no jurisdiction. There he told me he could promise me I could give a show.

Very gladly did I avail myself of his kindness, and we soon had our show on the new pitch. But I found that Peasenholme, if somewhat less narrow in its views than York itself, had its little peculiarities in the way of restrictions on showmen. We were just ready to sally forth to attract an audience – myself in my Hamlet's dress, my wife in her spangled finery, Hilyard, the clown, in his motley, and two others in fancy costumes – when a policeman came into the show and said, "If you wear any costumes except those that are the recognized ones of this country, man or woman, I have orders to arrest you."

So off came the dresses that we considered would be so attractive, and with sinking hearts, for we thought business would be spoiled, we put on the black garments we had provided for our mournful duties at Houghton-le-Spring, and thus sombrely arrayed opened our show. But "God and good angels fought on our side," as Shakespeare says, and to our astonishment and delight we took over twelve pounds.

I thought since we had done so well that I would stop on Peasenholme pitch for another day. But it appeared that the superintendent of the York police in plain clothes had been present at one of our performances, and when I went out into the street shortly afterwards he said, "The Lord Mayor," for the Chief Magistrate of York takes that title, which was conferred by Richard II, "wants to see you at once. Come along!"

I followed him in fear and trembling, wondering what new trouble was to befall me, and very soon was face to face with his lordship, who said, "You belong to the show upon Peasenholme, don't you?" I answered in the affirmative, and then he said: "Part of your entertainment is called the 'Suspension by Ether,' I am told. You administer the drug to a boy, and this gentleman on my left, who is a medical man, and also the superintendent informs me that such a performance is an outrage and cruelty on the child, and must eventually result in his death."

When I heard this I couldn't help smiling. "Oh, dear no, your lordship," I said. "The whole thing is a simple trick. There is no ether used, and there is certainly no danger nor cruelty to the boy." At this they stared, and asked for an explanation, and were mightily amused when they learned the secret of one of my most mystifying tricks – one which was then quite new, and always astounded the audience. It was simply this:–

Anaesthetics had begun at this time to revolutionize surgery, and the popular imagination was deeply stirred by the sleep-producing powers of chloroform and ether. That gave us conjurers an idea: we would send a boy to sleep in mid-air. A light but rigid steel frame was procured that fitted to one side of the boy's body, and when extended would support it from a joint at the boy's elbow. The frame, concealed beneath a loose dress, made no difference to the boy's movements on the stage.

He walked on, then there was a little mummery and patter about the wonder-working powers of ether. A bottle was produced, presumably containing the magic spirit, but really with nothing more dangerous in it than limpid pump water. A little manipulation with some of this on a handkerchief, and hey, presto! the boy falls back apparently asleep, and in a condition in which he seemingly becomes rigid and allows his limbs to be placed in any position at the will of the operator. The elbow is crooked, the concealed joint of the frame in the loose sleeve slips into the top of a pedestal that stands in the middle of the stage, and there is the boy, his cheek resting on his hand, sweetly asleep, full length in mid-air, with no other apparent support than his elbow on the pedestal.

The trick has become a very common one in these days, mesmeric passes taking the place of the supposed ether, with many variations introduced. It used to be shown as the Fakir of Oolu, and was for a time an Egyptian Hall sensation.

The Lord Mayor, the superintendent, and the doctor were amazed at the real simplicity of the mysterious trick, and promised not to expose it. Moreover, when, after asking permission, I had shown them some of my sleight-of-hand tricks, the Lord Mayor asked: "How long did you purpose staying in York?" "Only to-day, your lordship," was my reply. "Would you like to come into the market-place?" was his next question. "I should be delighted," I answered. "Very well, then," he said, "you may come and remain till the end of the week, and we will not charge you anything for your stand."

Here was a bit of luck and no mistake, and it sent my spirits up with a rush. We very soon pitched our show in the market-place, and the people having heard of my interview with the Lord Mayor hastened to patronize it. The Archbishop's lady and family and many leading people came to see us, and we did splendid business.

From York we went on through the Midland towns, reaching Grantham on the following Saturday, and starting early the next morning we reached Corby, in Lincolnshire, at nine o'clock on Sunday night. Misfortune we soon found had not done with us.

One of our horses died soon after our arrival, and we had to buy another at a cost of eighteen pounds. It was now the depth of winter and dreadful weather. For a whole week we had no chance of giving a show, and as I, never dreaming about having to buy another horse, had sent small sums of money away to three or four places to pay some debts, the Sunday following the one on which we reached Corby found us dead broke. We wanted to go on, but there was a toll-gate at the end of the village, and our whole company could not muster enough cash to pay the toll of one shilling and threepence. I offered the collector a Chinese gong, worth three or four pounds, as security. But no, he "deedn't onderstond they things," and "must 'ave th' munny afore the gate were opened."

What to do I did not know, but as we were bewailing our position we met a clergyman with his wife and four children. "What have you to exhibit in the caravan?" asked his reverence. I did not venture to mention conjuring, but told him of the performing hares, birds, and mice which I still carried with me. "Could you show them to the children?" he asked." Certainly," said I, and the parson led us to a small public-house. Watty Hilyard ran off and fetched the animals, and for a good half-hour or more I entertained that family party with their antics on the taproom table. When I had finished this best of parsons put his hand in his pocket and gave me ten shillings. "Made again, George!" said I to myself.

But trouble was still with us. Our horses had been put in the carriages, and we were just about to journey on, when our little boy, who had been ailing some time, was seized with a convulsive fit and passed away. There was nothing for it but to go on, so with tears streaming down our faces we washed and laid out the tiny body on a shutter in the living-carriage, and travelled forward to Stamford. There on the Monday, although it snowed very heavily, we turned out on parade, for we wanted the money to pay the funeral expenses of our firstborn. I shall never forget the experience. There in the bitter grey weather, our hearts as heavy as lead, we had to mount jests and smile to win the people to our show so that our loved one might be laid decently to rest. I wonder what the chaffing crowd would have thought could it have seen the sad thoughts that were hidden under our gay exteriors. But the mummer must smile though his heart be breaking, and so we went on, eventually winning enough for our purpose, and laying our babe in a tiny grave in the solemn God's acre attached to the church of St. Mary.

It was a doleful situation, and as the weather was still bad we were compelled to remain a second day. Then we went on a little way, and the weather clearing up, we again donned our finery, and at a village feast were blessed by taking between three and four pounds. That was a very dark period in my career; in fact, though I was not then to know it, the darkest hour before the dawn, for the next turn of Fortune's wheel was to put me on the upgrade on the road to an assured position.

# CHAPTER XXXII

## A LUCKY TOUR GIVES ME MY FIRST CIRCUS

AFTER my misfortunes in Lincolnshire the luck seemed to turn, and we did very well on the road, managing to get to London for the Easter holidays in excellent fettle and with a little cash in hand. So we went once more to Stepney Fair, of pleasant memories, and erected our booth against the "Maid and Magpie" public-house.

Novelty was what the public had begun to crave for, and no matter how stupid or exaggerated an announcement might be put up on a booth, if it only advertised something new there was sure to be a rush to see it. Of course, in nine cases out of ten the novelty seekers met with a disappointment, but they rarely made a noise about it, for they liked to see others gulled as well as themselves, so the game went merrily on.

Seeing that such a demand for novelty existed I felt it incumbent on me, as a showman counted amongst the smartest in the profession, to do what I could to satisfy the demand. So I set my wits to work and soon found some items to catch the public fancy. The first was, as I grandiloquently called it, my "Shoal of Trained Fish in their Exhibition of a Naval Engagement." That sounds big, doesn't it? Now for the facts as to size and character, for, as I promised at the beginning, I am going to tell you all my little secrets.

Well, then, I bought a glass tank, 2 feet 6 inches wide, 6 inches deep, and 6 feet 9 inches long; a number of goldfish, and some little toy boats such as were sold to children at a penny each. Into the boats I put some fine masts and spars with paper sails, and to each boat attached a fine steel wire, which went through the bottom about 3 inches and ended in a small noose. By just tickling the goldfish with a fine twig or a feather they could easily be made to put their heads into the wire nooses and to push the boats with them as they swam. It was astonishing to see how the fish would swim when their heads were noosed, carrying the boats up and down the tank at a rare rate. A small squib was attached to each mast and lit up, the parks flying as the startled fish darted hither and thither, and the naval engagement, with plenty of smoke and small detonations, was complete. "Simple," you will say. Quite so, but it was none the less very effective, and the people who came to see it were not only satisfied, but considered it a very clever exhibition.

My big hit, however, was made by my tame oyster. This was quite my own idea, and puzzled and amazed not only the public, but at its start the other showmen, who became quite envious of the novel attraction. It was a daring thing to do, but the result quite justified my audacity, though it was not without some qualms that I prepared a piece of calico, four yards long by a yard wide, and painted on it the legend: "The Only Novelty in the Fair. The Wonderful Performing Fish and a Tame Oyster that sits by the fire and smokes his yard of clay." How they did bite at this! My show was crowded as it had never been before.

Now, having let you into the secret of the performing fish, I'll let you into the secret of the tame oyster that smoked a pipe.

I had prepared a fine big oyster shell, the two halves fitting closely together as though it was a nice fresh bivalve. Inside were fixed two little pieces of piping opening to two holes in the lip of the oyster shell. These pipes were connected with two pieces of black rubber tubing that ran down under my conjuring table on the raised platform.

I had handy two or three nice fresh oysters that in appearance and size closely matched the dummy shell, which, laid on a dark grey cloth, was not visible to the audience. When all was ready I took one of my good oysters, and introducing it as "The Tame Oyster, the only one in the world!" handed it round, so that the company could see there was "no deception." When I got the oyster back I pretended to place it in the grey cloth, but really dropped it at the back of the table, while I pulled forward the prepared shell. This I lifted up on to a black bottle, with the two tubes running down behind well out of sight. Then, calling attention to the fact that everybody could see the oyster, I would get a clay pipe, put some tobacco in it, and then with a request to the oyster, "Now, sir, let the company see that you really are trained and intelligent by showing how you can smoke a pipe!" I would insert the stem of the pipe into the hole made for it in the shell, call a boy from the audience, give him a spill, and ask him to light the tobacco. As he did so, my boy who used to do the "Suspension by Ether," and who was concealed under the table, would draw the smoke down one tube and blew it back through the other, so that it really looked as though the oyster was puffing away at his pipe.

The trick never failed to amaze as well as amuse, more especially when, as if considering the oyster had smoked enough, I would say, "That will do, sir! You will make your head ache if you smoke too much!" With this I took the pipe away, and threw the corner of the grey cloth over the prepared oyster, at the same moment pulling the latter off the bottle and dropping it, tubes and all, into the drawer at the table back while I deftly substituted a real oyster. Then, throwing the corner of the cloth back, I would say, "There he is, ladies and gentlemen! Looks none the worse for his smoke, I think, but see for yourselves!" And the real oyster was handed round again, all believing it to be the one that had just been smoking. They used to go away quite convinced that they had seen an oyster enjoying a smoke and that there was "no deception."

Well, the "Tame Oyster," the "Performing Fish," the "Suspension by Ether," and several other new tricks, proved such an attraction that we took more money from Stepney Fair than we had ever imagined possible, and I resolved to try my luck with the same show in the West of England at the many fairs and regattas then held there.

This proved another good move. The jade Fortune was evidently now determined to be as kind as she had before been cruel, and money came in so fast that by September there was enough in hand to enable us to start on a venture, long before determined on as likely if we could only get a fair start, to bring us better returns than any other class of show. This was a circus, and a circus we accordingly arranged to have without delay.

Our first purchase to this end was made at Croydon October Fair in the shape of a Welsh pony, for which we gave seven pounds. I soon taught him, with a little variation of the method I have described as used in training the learned pig, to do the talking, fortune-telling, and card-picking business. Then we moved on to Norwich, and there, through the winter, in the grounds of a public-house by the river-side that afforded accommodation for the enterprise, set to work to prepare our show-front, forty-five feet in length and twenty-eight feet in height, that was to adorn the big tent we were having made for us.

I will not say that as a work of art our show-front would have secured a place in the Royal Academy, but it caught the eyes of the country people amazingly, and I was very proud of it, for it was practically my own. I used to spend about six hours of each day in painting, and the rest, sometimes up to twelve o'clock at night, with my brother John, teaching the circus business to two nieces, one nephew, and four other youngsters I had taken as apprentices. In my time I have taught some twenty youngsters, who have all become not only firstclass and very successful artistes, but most of them managers and proprietors.

With the spring our circus was in a fair way of completion, and I resolved to open at King's Lynn at the great Charter Fair, which always commenced on February 14th, and lasted six days. So down to the grand old town on the east bank of the Ouse we made our way, and put up the new show, with its pictures illustrating the greatest impossibilities it is possible to conceive.

But they served their turn admirably, and when we – that is to say, myself; my nieces, nephew, and apprentices; Watty Hilyard, the famous clown; John Croueste, the noted general performer; and William Kite, who came of a wonderful circus family, and could do almost any ring business you could mention – strutted forth before the public gaze, in tights and trunks, everybody, including even the showmen, was impressed and astonished.

I had bought for eighteen pounds another good horse, which was ridden from London to Norwich by John Croueste, and we had trained it to gallop circus fashion in a proper forty-two feet ring in the public-house yard. All the time the fair lasted we were practising when we were not performing, and we speedily became very proficient.

We made money at King's Lynn, and, what was better, went on making it at the fairs we took in the Lincoln, Cambridge, Norfolk, and Suffolk district, while we were waiting for the great Eastertide Fair at Norwich. At this time, remember, our prices were a penny admission, with threepence for reserved seats.

On our way to Norwich Fair at Long Sutton, a mere village, we did what is known in the profession as "Blank Moulding." On a wide space in the turnpike road we put down a few seats and something in the shape of a ring, made up a few of the old-fashioned grease-pot lights with tallow and rags for wicks, and announced a grand performance. There was no charge to view the latter, as the ring was perfectly open, but we charged a penny each to all who wanted a seat.

We presented a lively little programme of juggling, rope-walking, trick-riding, etc., and when half-way through it, in order to get our expenses, called a rest, during which the following bit of patter was indulged in: "Now, ladies and gentlemen, you know we are not doing this for our own amusement, but we thought as we were resting here tonight we would give you a little enjoyment. In order to test your appreciation of our efforts, before we go on with the rest of the performance the young men will go round with the hat." This is known in the profession as "nobbing," and not a soul among the spectators, some two or three hundred, escaped being "nobbed," whether they parted or not. Then the second part of the performance was proceeded with.

The last item was my fortune-telling pony, who did very well until I came to the finish. This always was to tell the pony to go round and find out the biggest rogue in the company. The proper response was to walk up to the ringmaster, so pointing him out as the biggest rogue in question. I never knew him do a wrong thing before, but on this occasion, after I had given him his order, and stood with my back to him waiting for him to come and push his head against me, I heard the people laughing.

Turning round, I saw the pony with his head resting on the shoulder of the village constable, who looked very red and unhappy. I at once threw the whip forward, driving the pony round the ring, at the same time saying, "You have made a mistake sir! I told you to find the biggest rogue in the company: try again!" and with this I gave him the usual cue.

But it was of no use. The pony, instead of coming up to me, merely walked some ten paces on, then turned and came back to the unfortunate constable, while the crowd shrieked with laughter. I was now really vexed, so I cracked the whip, and the pony came up to me, while I said, giving him the knee cue, "You have been very rude to that gentleman; down on your knees, sir, to beg pardon for your mistake." But the crowd wouldn't have it. "No, no," they shouted; "pony knows better than you! Pony's all right! He made no mistake, he didn't! Us know pleeceman, and so do pony, it appears!" Here the laughter and the jeering broke out afresh, and we had to leave the matter where it stood.

The constable, however, was a very good fellow, and he came in with the rest afterwards and made a joke of it, for we had quite a gala night in the village, myself and company sitting among our patrons drinking four ale and smoking long pipes. The collection was a very good one, too; in fact, our bit of "blank moulding" quite paid expenses, besides making us some new friends, and giving us an excellent advertisement.

We did so well that at Manchester Whit-Monday Fair we had increased our stud to nine horses and two ponies. I resolved after Manchester to make for Scotland, travelling through the Lake District, and at the little town of Keswick, at the fair held there on August 2nd, we made our first rise of prices, making admission threepence and reserved seats sixpence. The occasion was the spectacle of "Mazeppa," which we had been rehearsing for some time, and nobody grumbled at the increased prices; in fact, everybody seemed to take them as the regular thing, and I saw that the new move was a good one. At Carlisle, which we reached in time for the great fair, held regularly on August 26th, we took with the new prices close upon a hundred pounds. Then I realized that we were fairly on the up-grade at last, that the way to competence, if not to fortune, was open to me.

Going to Scotland I found I had over five hundred pounds in hand, and on the way to Glasgow I bought thirteen more horses, all of them handsome and well coloured, and an extra pony. We then changed the programme, and with it the prices again, making them now sixpence, one shilling, and two shillings. At Glasgow for five weeks we had an enormous run, and then we moved on, doing splendid business, for in Scotland a circus was then quite a novelty. Dundee, Paisley, Kirnham, Greenock, Aberdeen, Edinburgh, and Inverness, where we were at the time of the Highland Games, fairly rose at us. I wintered in South Shields, where I became a great favourite with the people, and felt that at last things were indeed looking rosy with me.

# CHAPTER XXXIII

## HOW BUCK-JUMPING HORSES ARE TRAINED

AFTER my summer tour in 1854 I took a large piece of ground in the very lowest part of Liverpool, Bannister Street, wherein was kept what was known as "Paddy's Market." I wanted to make wintering pay, and I thought I saw my way to it. So I built a large show, with boarded sides and a canvas top, the place holding at one penny each admission about four pounds. Here we had a semi-dramatic cum-circus sort of entertainment that exactly suited the neighbourhood.

Really, the circus formed but a small portion of the show, though we kept ourselves fit for the road by two hours' practice every morning. What we mostly did was acting on the gaff principle, and there was nothing we were afraid to tackle in the dramatic line, from Shakespeare downwards. For twenty-three weeks we gave three performances a night with a change of piece each evening, always to full houses.

At this time Mr. W. Cooke had a splendid company at the Amphitheatre with Wallett and others, but though salaries paid to artistes in those days were very small, his venture proved a failure, and a good many of his performers drifted to my cross-bred affair in Bannister Street. Later on in the same year Lambert and Lambert's Russian Company came to the Amphitheatre with the same disastrous result, and one by one all their company figured at my penny show.

One of our best and most popular actors in Bannister Street was Bill Matthews. He was a good rider, tumbler, vaulter: and clown; in fact, an excellent all-round performer. His wife, too, was a splendid little woman. She was our leading lady, and very clever; she was otherwise remarkable, too, for she had twenty-one children, all alive and active. The family have since been well known as the Matthews Family, the Sisters Matthews especially being great favourites at the theatres and circuses, both at home and abroad.

Bill Matthews made a big hit this winter, which was the terrible one of the Crimean War, by his impersonation of Paddy Kelly, an

Irishman who had distinguished himself as a soldier at the Alma, news of which battle, fought on September 20th, had thrilled the nation. Well, Matthews did a riding act, "Paddy Kelly, the hero of the Russian War," and in his uniform, slashing at the enemy with a sword and plentiful dabs from a sponge of rose-pink, excited the audience to frenzy.

Having achieved such a success in Scotland previously we made that country our summer touring ground again with equally good results. "Mazeppa; or, the Wild Horse of Tartary," was still our great draw. It was a novelty then in the provinces, and people never seemed to tire of it. We have heard much of late years of buck-jumping horses which the persuasive American would have the people believe a natural product that can only be mastered by the cowboy. Bunkum, my friends – bunkum pure and simple!

The fiery, untamed steed which so delighted the Scotch audiences was a decent-looking spotted horse which had seen quite twenty summers and winters. I bought him from an Irishman near Liverpool, and broke him to the business of rearing, kicking, bucking, and to the seeming tumble-down-from-sheer-exhaustion which is a feature of the Mazeppa show. How I did it I will tell you.

To make a good kicking, rearing, or buck-jumping horse for Mazeppa or Buffalo Bill business the chief instrument you require is an ordinary pin. When you approach the horse put your hand against the pommel of the saddle, near his withers, and prick him sharply there with the pin. The animal at once rears up. Directly he does so, caress him to show him he is doing what you want him to do. Repeat this process a few times, and the horse will rear to the tap of the finger without the pin, and, what is more, he never forgets the lesson. To make a horse fling up from behind the pin the process is repeated at the back of the saddle on the crupper. A few simultaneous touches on crupper and withers together produce the buck-jump.

In this way you might within a week produce a hundred fiery, untamed steeds if you happened to want them.

Training the horse to lie down at command is a little more tedious. You strap up the off fore-leg, and then with a light hand-whip or fine cane gently tap him below the knee on the fore-leg on which he stands. To avoid this treatment the horse will presently go to his knees. When he does that, caress him to show him he has done the right thing.

When you have done this a few times, if you go to the off side and pull the bridle towards you, the horse will lean on the near side and lie down, and on the lesson being repeated a few times he soon learns your wishes and becomes efficient in his business. Always remember one thing: never lose your temper with the animal, and in the end you will find that you can without any unkind treatment teach him to do anything you want him to do.

There was only one thing I had to complain about in the spotted Mazeppa steed I have mentioned. With a travelling circus you have all weathers to put up with, and very often if there had been much rain the ring was ankle-deep in mud. Whenever it was so that old horse would make for the wettest, softest spot for the lying-down act. As I played Mazeppa, my feelings in this uncomfortable situation, while the Khan rapped out his rather long speech, "Whence is this wounded and exhausted stranger," etc., may be imagined. I never quite got used to this mud bath, though I have played the part of Mazeppa in my own and other establishments upwards of nine thousand times.

# CHAPTER XXXIV

## I BEAT THE YANKEES AND BECOME PROPRIETOR OF ASTLEY'S

SEASON after season was now a record of success with us, and the establishment grew steadily, but I was ambitious and anxious to show that if I had the opportunity I could do yet bigger things. My chance came in 1856, when Howe and Cushing's great American Show landed in Liverpool, bringing, amongst other things, a company of Red Indians. I went to see the first performance of the much-billed combination, which was to eclipse all English circuses, and, to my surprise, found that one of the Indian chiefs was a man who had been with me some twelve years before. I had picked him up in Ratcliff Highway, and he was a very ordinary specimen of an African negro.

"Ho! ho!" said I to myself, is that how it's done?" and then, I blush to say it, for the first time in my life I set to work to copy another man's ideas." I want some savages," I said to a Liverpool detective, who was a friend of mine. "Very well," he said; "come along with me." I did, and we went into some dreadful slums, where in half an hour I engaged eight wild men and two savage women. One of the men was, I think, the most awful-looking fellow I ever saw, so I made him chief of the tribe.

A little red ochre for skin tint, some long, snaky black hair, feathers, skins, and beads did the trick properly, and I had as savage a lot of Ojibbeways to look at as ever took a scalp. They had some terrible-looking weapons, and learned to do war dances, to yell like fiends, and to perform tribal ceremonies. They lived, or were supposed to, in an iron-barred carriage for safety's sake, and I would walk them out before the grand procession and make an impression by buying them fruit and sweetmeats. My! it was a swindle, and now and again my conscience troubled me fearfully about it, but when I thought of Howe and Cushing I always felt justified.

I was, too, for my American rivals had advertising agents over-billing every other circus, whether they were going into the same town or not. My bills were out for Perth, when down came the great American

Eagle with its unscrupulous methods and blotted them out with the flaring Yankee posters. I could see the way to make this play my game, so I took no notice beyond postponing the date of my coming to Perth. Then I had the American advertisement from *The Scotsman* copied and arranged so as to fit my establishment, while people reading it would be puzzled to know whether it was the colossal Yankee show or not. When this was done on I went.

At this time we had over sixty horses, a troupe of twelve genuine Arabs, my special Indian savages, a splendid band, and a company of circus artistes who were the very foremost in their profession. Whether the people confounded us with the genuine American show or not I cannot say, but we gave unbounded satisfaction wherever we went in Scotland and scooped the pool. I wintered in Nicholson Street, Edinburgh, in a fine building, for three months, and did immense business.

I now resolved to add wild animals to my attraction – so I bought six lions in London from Mr. Jamrach, and soon got them trained for the summer campaign. They took part in a little scena I prepared, called "The Condemned Preserved," in which a Rajah condemns a poor African boy who has dared to love his daughter to be torn to death by lions. When the boy (myself) was cast into the den, in the confusion the Rajah's daughter (Mrs. George Sanger) follows her lover amongst the beasts. Then the Rajah cries, "My child! Who will save my child" and of course the African lover does the saving, quells the savage lions, and the relenting father receives him as a son. It used to bring the house down!

Every week now we added something to the show in the way of wild beasts, and in 1871, when I bought Astley's Amphitheatre in the Westminster Bridge Road from the widow of Mr. William Batty for £11,000, the menagerie was an integral part of the establishment, and was considered the largest and best in England.

It was in November, 1871, that my deal with Mrs. Batty was completed, and just before this I had taken a three years' lease of the Agricultural Hall, Islington, for a circus and spectacular exhibition. I had also built circuses in Manchester, where I kept a show going five years continuously, and in Birmingham, Liverpool, Glasgow, Dundee, Aberdeen, Bath, Bristol, Exeter, and Plymouth. The poor little peep-show boy had indeed grown up.

Astley's, of course, was a great venture. It was the historical English home of the riders of the ring. Founded in 1780 by Philip Astley, who had been a light horseman with General Elliott's regiment, and who was presented, amongst other things, with a performing charger in recognition of his gallantry in action, it had a reputation as a circus that was worldwide – a reputation that it was no light task to properly keep up.

But if it made reputations, it did not make fortunes. Prior to my acquiring it, Dion Boucicault had had it, reconstructed it, and went bankrupt. William Cooke rented it from Mr. Batty, and lost £16,000 in it. Jim Harwood, the great impersonator of Dick Turpin, failed there and nearly broke his heart. That great showman, E. T. Smith, who had Cremorne Gardens, ran Astley's two or three years, and came to utter grief, I knew all this, but all the same did not lose confidence, with the result that I ran the theatre successfully over twenty years, eight years longer than any lessee had ever done before me, and kept up its high reputation to the last. It is really one of the few things in my life that I am very proud of and inclined to boast about.

Directly I got the place I determined to enlarge, modernize and beautify it, and the work, commenced on November 2nd, 1871, was carried out by Mr. Robinson, who afterwards became architect to the Lord Chamberlain. Mr. Matcham, the now famous theatrical architect, married one of Mr. Robinson's daughters, and one of the very first pieces of work he did was to design certain improvements and alterations at Astley's.

The work, despite a strike, was hurried on, and at Christmas I was enabled to open with my first spectacular pantomime, "Lady Godiva." I had worked out the situations for this myself, and indeed practically wrote the book. Miss Amy Sheridan, considered at that time the finest woman on the stage, was the Godiva, and the piece, a combination of stage and ring, the legitimate and the equestrian drama with an introduction of all sorts of wild animals, proved an enormous success, and drew all London to see it.

As a little boy I had been taken to Astley's by my father, and sitting in the gallery, entranced by the performance, I thought I would give the world to become the proprietor of such a show. On the Boxing Night of 1871 I remembered this visit and desire of mine as I looked round the brilliant crowded house of which I was now the owner. I had achieved another of my ambitions, and my heart went out in thankfulness to the Providence that had been so kind to me, while at the same time there was a dash of sorrow in my cup of joy, inasmuch that my dearly loved parents had not lived to share it with me.

# CHAPTER XXXV
## JOHN AND I DISSOLVE PARTNERSHIP

ABOUT the very time I entered into possession of Astley's – namely, the last months of 1871 – a great shadow and anxiety fell upon the Queen and nation in the shape of the serious illness of the Prince of Wales, now our beloved King, from typhoid fever. After his happy recovery, her Majesty, in gratitude to the all-merciful Power, arranged thanksgiving services and festivities, including a grand State progress through London.

I was very anxious to take part in that Royal pageant, and as I was very good friends with the police authorities it was arranged that if I liked to organize a procession of my own on the great day, following not too close upon the Royal procession, it would not be interfered with.

That was good enough for me, and I spent over £7,000 in making and preparing everything necessary to do honour to the occasion and credit to my own name. Starting the procession from the Agricultural Hall, I rode in advance, and at the top of Tottenham Court Road, which was the point at which we proposed to drop in behind the Royal procession, we were stopped by mounted police, the crowds surging about us in all directions and closing up behind.

Then took place a little bit of rehearsed by-play between myself and the police. The superintendent in charge rode forward and exclaimed, "What are you doing here? What are you doing here?" Then, in a louder voice, "Go back! Go back directly!"

But the crowd was so dense there was no going back, and the people swayed and pushed, while they yelled and cheered at the top of their voices. At last the superintendent rode to the front again, and, coming close to my side, gave me a wink, and then shouted, "You can't get back, so you must go forward, Sanger! Go forward; it's all right. We shall hold you responsible! Get along!"

With that I took off my hat, bowed right and left, and on we went. Our show drew forth tremendous cheering, for its tinsel finery had a great deal more glitter about it than the solid grandeur of the Royal procession. We had our Britannia, Mrs. George Sanger with her living lion on the top to typify the nation and its strength. The Queen, too, was impersonated, in her crown and robes, surrounded by representatives of her dominions, all in correct costume. At the top of Park Lane there were about a dozen carriages that had fallen out of the Royal procession, and as our mimic pageant came along the occupants of these carriages, amongst whom Lord Beaconsfield was conspicuous, rose and acknowledged the endeavour of your humble servant to enhance the circumstance of the great occasion. A further acknowledgment was accorded me by my being included among the favoured individuals who received tickets for two seats to take part in the imposing ceremony at St. Paul's Cathedral.

It was a great honour and a great triumph for me, bringing from all parts of the country expressions of a desire to see Sanger's Royal Thanksgiving Procession, and I reproduced it faithfully afterwards at many places in the provinces. The Peel Park (Bradford) Committee at once seized upon the opportunity and engaged my company for their great Whitsun fete. I made the necessary arrangements and the affair was an overwhelming success.

On the Monday we had 80,000 visitors, and on the Tuesday 96,000 passed the turnstiles, this being the largest concourse of people ever assembled in one day to witness such a performance.

The next event of my career was the dissolving of the partnership with my brother John. We had worked well together with every possible success, but the families of each of us were growing rapidly, and each of us thought it would be best if we had separate establishments. So we agreed to divide our possessions, and did so in the simplest and most amicable way possible. Certain things were already my sole property, certain things were John's sole property. For the rest we knew exactly what there was, what everything was worth. So we went into the stable-yard attached to the Amphitheatre in the Westminster Bridge Road and tossed with a shilling for each article. The winner of the toss took the goods and paid over half their value to the loser, or took the half-value and handed over the goods, just which he chose, each of us tossing in turn.

For instance, we had an elephant, Old Jennie, which we valued at £1,200. I won the toss, took Jennie, and gave John a cheque for £600. In this way we divided property worth considerably over £100,000 without any bickering or trouble, each being quite satisfied and contented. It was a quick, comfortable way of doing business, if a somewhat unusual one, and I doubt very much if the

Westminster Bridge Road has witnessed either before or since a tossing match on such a scale or for such stakes.

So John started with the big circus company, which his sons, keeping up in every way the Sanger reputation, are still running as John Sanger, Limited. I paid him out a minor interest which he had in Astley's and the Agricultural Hall, and we went our separate business ways, remaining, however, the best of good friends and brothers until his death.

# CHAPTER XXXVI

## ON THE CONTINENT: AN ADVENTURE

SANGER was a name now so well known in England as to be almost a household word, and I resolved to make it wider known yet by a tour on the Continent. For this tour I took forty-six carriages, 160 horses, eleven elephants, twelve camels, all sorts of circus accessories and 230 people.

For the shipment of this lot from Deptford to Havre I paid a steamship company £1,200. For this money they found me what I all too late discovered to be a worn-out cattle-boat that had been laid up for some time, and was so shaky that when the captain saw the amount of rolling stock and live plant on the upper deck he hesitated to put to sea.

At last, however, he started, the old boat pitching and rolling in a frightful manner. She did not improve as she went on, and when we had been two hours out the captain gave orders to heave-to. When I asked him the meaning of this he said the boat, with such a deck-load, was so unsteady that he thought it would be best not to risk the passage, but to return to Deptford.

I strongly objected to this, and told him that as it was a fine night he had better go on. He reminded me that my show, with all its people and animals, was not insured for a single penny. I said this was quite true, but as I was prepared to take the risk he must proceed. My persistence had its effect, and very unwillingly he went on, with the result that we travelled through a bright windless moonlight night without mishap, and reached Havre at eight in the morning in a dead calm.

No sooner had we got alongside the quay, though, than one of the worst storms I have ever experienced broke out with a suddenness that took everybody by surprise. The shipping in the harbour was tossed and beaten about, and broken from anchorage in a way terrible to witness. Our old boat was dashed again and again against the side of the quay, where thousands of people, in consequence of our advertisement, had assembled to witness our arrival. Quite an army of gendarmes, firemen, and dock labourers, headed by the mayor, came to our help in making fast this wretched boat. Steamers, with check-lines attached, tried to steady her action, whilst on board the shrieking of the women and children, the trumpeting of the elephants, the screaming of horses thrown from their feet and trampling each other on the deck, made up a babel of horrid noises such as I never heard the like of before, and most sincerely trust I may never hear again.

Seven hours the gale and panic continued, and not an animal could be taken off the whole day. The captain and mate were badly injured, and when the weather quieted down had to be taken to the hospital. After much difficulty my company, animals, and belongings were all safely landed amid the cheers of the thousands of people who had congregated, in addition to the first sightseers, to watch our battle against destruction. They also loudly condemned the action of the steamship company in jeopardizing our lives and property by placing us on such a worn-out vessel.

I visited the captain in hospital, and he looked much more a wreck than his old boat. He was thoroughly broken up, and his words to me were: "I may get over my injuries, but I shall never get my nerve back. Had we had the slightest sea on the passage not a creature would have ever trod the land again." The incident was reported in every French paper, with the result that, as out of sadness, cometh joy. The advertisement gained by it meant crowded business all through our French tour – two performances every week-day and three on Sunday – for I had to conform to the Continental Sabbath customs, though I did not like doing so.

I had eleven summers through France, Germany, Austria, Bohemia, Spain, Switzerland, Denmark, and Holland. I have played in all their capitals, and have been honoured by the patronage of ten crowned heads.

# CHAPTER XXXVII

## "THE LIONS ARE LOOSE!"

OF course, I had many adventures and encounters in these Continental journeys, but two particularly stand out in my memory.

One of these experiences was in 1876, when I was in France, and the proprietor of the Porte St. Martin Theatre in Paris sought me out at Clermont-Ferraud. He told me he was about to produce for the second time *Round the World in Eighty Days*, and as he had seen a coloured man performing with eight lions at the circus he thought they might effectively be introduced into the play in a love scene which takes place in an African forest.

Well, he engaged the lions at a salary of £320 a month, and I undertook to provide the scene for what was really a fine and exciting situation. This effective scene, representing a piece of forest, was what is professionally known as a cut cloth, reaching the full width of the stage. Instead, however, of being made of ordinary theatrical material, it was composed of gas-piping, bent in every conceivable form, and varying in thickness from three inches to half an inch. To this framing was attached the painted foliage cut from sheet iron, the whole being put close enough together to prevent the lions getting through, though they and their surroundings were all clearly visible to the spectators. It was all made from my designs by my gas engineer at the Amphitheatre in the Westminster Bridge Road, and was delayed in its transit from London to Paris till two days before the production of the piece, so that no rehearsal with the scene in position was possible.

As for the lions, I did not want to part with those that were travelling with my circus, so having another group at Margate, where I had purchased the Hall-by-the-Sea and the Kitchen Garden from the London, Chatham and Dover Railway Company, I resolved to use the latter. I therefore went to England, boxed up the lions in wooden cages, and sent them with all speed to Paris. With them I sent two men, keepers in my Zoo at Margate, Walter Stratford and W. Pitcher.

The lions arrived in Paris on the Friday morning, the production being fixed for the Sunday, and as everything was behind, including the fixing of the iron forest, it was decided that there should be no rehearsal with the animals until Saturday. In the meantime the lions were lowered into a cellar under the stage.

I was very early astir on the Saturday in order to rehearse the lions before very many people were about. Directly I got in sight of the theatre, however, I was astonished to see a crowd about it. As I drew nearer I could see there were a lot of gendarmes present, and also my two men from Margate. When they caught sight of me they rushed forward with faces white as wax, Stratford wringing his hands and crying, "Oh, Guv'nor! Guv'nor! The lions are loose!"

"Loose!" I exclaimed; "what do you mean?" "They are loose from their dens," he replied," and this gentleman here," pointing to a gendarme officer, "says they must be shot in the interest of public safety."

"Oh no," I said to the gendarme, "no shooting, please." Then, turning to my fellows, I said, "Come along! Come along! Let us get them into the dens!" To my surprise they did not budge. "Come along!" I said again; "aren't you coming?" But I got no response, so with a few unkindly remarks as to their want of pluck, I took the oil lamp from the watchman, who had been on duty at the theatre, and told him to unlock the stage-door.

When he had done so, I entered alone, the oil lamp in one hand and an ordinary walking-stick in the other. I rambled all over the theatre stage, dress-circle, pit, etc., and finding no trace of the lions concluded they were still in the cellar. With the dim light I had it was difficult to find my way about, but down I went, and not seeing them in the upper cellar crossed over to descend to the lower one. As I did so a lion suddenly made a rush for the same opening, and as he came struck me with his head in the small of the back with such force as to make me turn a complete somersault.

I landed on my feet, thanks to my old circus experience, but I confess that for the moment I was unnerved. The lantern, however, was still in my hand, and still burning, so after collecting my thoughts I descended the steps to the lower cellar. Then I made for the spot on which the dens had been placed. There was a great deal of old scenery, rubbish, and cast-off properties about, so I very carefully made the round of the cellar, picking my way at every step.

All at once I saw eyes like balls of fire in the distant darkness. "Oh, there you are, you rascals!" I shouted, knowing that the animals would recognize my voice. Then I struck my cane on the various properties lying about, and at the same time swung the lantern to and fro. This had the effect of making the eight lions leap and bound in all directions. The rattle of the old canvas and other material that was thrown over by the heavy beasts, together with their surprise at my appearance, made them run round the cellar several times. By this time I was quite awake to the situation. I knew from experience that the beasts would make for their dens when they tired a bit. So it proved, for presently after another race round they made for the cases they had escaped from. I saw three get into one of the great boxes, and five into another, leaving two empty. Then I pushed to and blocked as well as I could the sliding doors of the cases, and hurried up to inform my men that the danger was over, and the lions were safely housed.

I got my men to come down, and while twelve gendarmes with rifles occupied the stage, we nailed up the cage doors, and made all secure for the time being. Then I went off to breakfast and to wait for the dress rehearsal.

This commenced at nine o'clock on the Saturday night, the house being filled by invited friends, Pressmen, the Mayor of Paris, and a host of important personages. From the stage the theatre presented quite an imposing appearance, and after the rehearsal of each scene the manager would walk forward and ask the spectators if they could suggest any improvement. Sometimes a suggestion was made, and the scene would be rehearsed again. All this meant delay, and so the thing went on till about three in the morning.

Before the forest scene with the lions was produced there was an interval of an hour for refreshments, and after this the whole theatre was agog with excitement. The dens containing the lions had to be craned out of the cellar at the last moment owing to the space required for the early part of the play. The den with the five lions was got up, and put at the back ready for use all right, but in lifting the box with the three lions the rope slipped, with the result that the animals were thrown against the makeshift door with such force that one of them fell out.

In an instant a scene-shifter who had been helping rushed up to the proprietor, who was on the stage by me, and in an excited whisper said: "The lions are loose! The lions are loose!" The director for a moment was speechless, then he threw himself into a chair quivering like a jelly. Then he caught hold of my hand and cried, "The lions are loose! My God! Do you hear? The lions are loose!"

I was quite collected, and said calmly, "All right, sir! All right! It will be all right!" "What!" he said, glaring at me. "What! All right! Don't you see I am ruined!" and he paced the stage like a madman. I saw that the lion had got back in his place again, and that the beasts were ready for the performance, and managed at last to bring the fact home to the director, greatly to his relief. Now came another shock. The coloured performer, the hero of the forest scene, was missing.

When he was found he was helpless. Admiring friends had been entertaining him not wisely but too well, and he could neither speak nor stand. I volunteered to pull the director out of this fresh hole, and finding my way to the dressing-rooms speedily blacked up for the part, and found a suitable wig and dress. The scene was now ready and on I went. There was only one drawback. I knew nothing whatever of the lines of the part, and as I was not a proficient French scholar could not have spoken them very well even if I had known them.

However, I "gagged" as best I could, while my fair companion in the scene spoke her part. At the proper moment came the roar of the lions, done by an ingenious instrument contrived for the purpose in case the lions did not roar when they were wanted to do so. The young actress took fright at the beasts, and I had a job to compose her in the lovemaking scene, after which she was led behind a small ironwork screen for safety. Then came the professional thunder and lightning, roaring and clamour, the lions being forced on to the stage at the back while with two nine-chambered revolvers I made them bound, snarl, and show their teeth, and some half-dozen men at the back kept up a rattle of revolver shots to work up the excitement.

In the finishing scene, a very thrilling one, the big lion, who was harmless as a dog, jumped when I stamped my foot, and put his fore-paws on my shoulders as he had been trained to do. Then I threw him off, and falling to the stage with him we rolled over together as if in combat, the lion at the end lying quite still as if dead, while I rose and put my foot on his body in an attitude of triumph.

How those Frenchmen yelled and screamed at this! They seemed to go mad with excitement. The curtain was lowered and raised again five times. At the last I prevailed upon the pretty young actress to come forward with me to the centre of the stage amongst the animals before the audience. As she did so she shook to such an extent that I found it almost impossible to support her. The applause was wonderful, the curtain fell for the fifth time, and as it did so I noticed that the fair cheek of my companion had a large patch of black upon it, gained when, in her fear of the lions, she had reclined her head upon my shoulder.

There was another interval of an hour, during which the lions were cleared away, and the Mayor, the Pressmen, and the notabilities came upon the stage. The manager was so delighted with the success that he kissed me in the Continental fashion upon both my black cheeks. All were agreed that the scene was magnificent. As it was now five in the morning, and there was another scene to be rehearsed which did not affect me, I made my exit, very tired indeed. I need only remark that with the real coloured man and my lions the piece ran sixteen months, making a fortune for the lucky and enterprising proprietor.

The other Continental experience which has so fixed itself on my memory occurred two years later, and was of quite a different kind. I was at Verviers, in Belgium, with my circus in 1878, at the time of the conclusion of the Berlin Treaty, when all the world was talking of the diplomacy of Lord Beaconsfield, and the manner in which he had upheld the glory and the honour of Old England.

Verviers was the first stopping-place of the train conveying the triumphant statesman home. Here was a chance to give him a welcome. I had some hundreds of new bunting flags, and with the assistance of my company and the Belgian authorities, who entered heartily into the scheme, we transformed the somewhat dingy station into quite a gay and festive-looking building.

My English band of twenty performers struck up "God Save the Queen" as the train steamed into the station, and as it drew up at the platform Lord Beaconsfield, with the signs of labour and fatigue upon his never-to-be-forgotten face, looked out of the window, and asked the stationmaster, "What band is that?"

The stationmaster replied, "It is an English band, my lord! It is the band of the circus belonging to Mr. Sanger here. He is the proprietor." The next minute the carriage door was opened, and there was the great statesman stretching out his hand, with the words, "I am very glad to see you, Mr. Sanger. I have often heard of you, and am very pleased to meet you! I knew it must be an English band!"

I stammered out a few words of thanks and a humble congratulation on the splendid manner in which he had served our country. This was met with a kindly smile and a good-humoured shake of the head. Then he gave another grip of the hand to myself and the stationmaster, and turned with a courtly bow to accept a basket of strawberries which a lady came up and offered him; while the band burst out with the strains of "The Conquering Hero," and the crowd of English residents and Belgian notabilities on the platform burst out cheering.

It was really a wonderful reception that was accorded to the great English statesman, not only by the British residents, but by the people of Verviers themselves. The cheering was frantic, ladies leading the way, some crying, some laughing, some singing the National Anthem. It was a welcome to touch any man, and as the train steamed out of the station there were tears on the cheeks of the wonderful diplomatist as he bowed and saluted from the window.

I have been asked whether I put up amongst other mottoes on that auspicious occasion the famous one of "Peace with Honour." I did not, the reason being that it did not come into existence till some few hours after Lord Beaconsfield's welcome at Verviers. It was at Calais that it first became current. At that seaport, Mr. Maclure, afterwards M.P., met Lord Beaconsfield in order to show him in advance the terms of a congratulatory address presented by the Conservatives of Lancashire. In that address was the phrase "Peace with Honour," which at once caught the fancy of the statesman, who gave it currency by repetition in his reply speech and in many speeches he delivered later.

# CHAPTER XXXVIII

## HOW I BECAME "LORD" GEORGE

Now, as the finish of my story is drawing near, I am going to tell for the first time exactly in what circumstances I acquired the title of Lord George Sanger, by which I am so widely known. As I said in the beginning of my reminiscences I was not, as so many persons have fondly imagined, christened "Lord," any more than I was born in Newbury Workhouse. But it did not suit me to contradict the various stories about the genesis of my title that were set floating, for the more people talked and wondered about me the better I was being advertised. Now you shall have the truth, the whole truth, and nothing but the truth.

Well, then, I was first announced as " Lord" George through the American invasion of our shores by the various big combination shows, more especially that of "Buffalo Bill." For some time prior to his arrival in England the latter had been making a big hit in the States with his Wild West Exhibition of Indian, Cowboy, and Prairie life generally. In books of adventure over here the name of the Hon. William Cody had for some years figured very extensively. He was held up as the typical scout and Indian fighter, and the stories of his exploits, apocryphal and otherwise, as "Buffalo Bill," were very popular.

I was never behind the times with my show if I could help it, and having one or two real buffaloes, a number of unreal Red Indians, some good mules, and a rickety stage coach, I made "Scenes from Buffalo Bill" one of the features of my circus and a standing line on the bill.

I had been running this performance some twelve months before "Buffalo Bill" and his "Wild West" came to England, and when he did come, and his agents played the usual American "enterprising" game of plastering over the bills of every rival show throughout the country, I determined, out of "sheer cussedness," as my Yankee friends put it, not to drop the feature.

Naturally, the Honourable William was annoyed with me, and at once sought the aid of the law to get "Buffalo Bill" off Sanger's bills.

With their usual hustling methods, his agents rushed into the courts, and on an entirely ex-parte statement secured an injunction against me forbidding me to use the name of "Buffalo Bill."

My lawyers, Messrs. Lewis and Lewis, advised me, as there had been certain irregularities, to take no notice of the injunctions; so I went on as before, announcing and giving the "Buffalo Bill" performance. The next move of the Americans was to try to get me committed to gaol for contempt of court, and I had to show up at the big building in the Strand to show cause why I should not be committed. There I met the Hon. William Cody. He went into the box, and I went into the box, and a very pretty display of contradictory statements resulted. After I had said what I had to say, I went off to Barnet, where my circus then was, to look after my business and await the result.

That reached me just towards the close of the afternoon performance, in the shape of a telegram to say I had won the day. I read that telegram to the audience, who cheered me heartily, and I promised to put the facts before them in a special bill.

As I was reading the evidence with a view to getting the bill ready, the continual reiteration of the phrase "The Honourable William Cody" got on my nerves, and at last I said, "Hang it! I can go one better than that, anyhow. If he's the *Honourable* William Cody, then I'm *Lord* George Sanger from this out!"

And so I have been. I remembered that in the old days my father would jokingly call me "his lordship," and somehow I liked the title. Therefore when the special bill came out it set forth the facts, line by line, in this way: "The Hon. W. Cody said so-and-so, and Lord George Sanger said so-and-so." The repetition of the name caught the public fancy. Wherever George Sanger appeared about my circus I painted "Lord" in front of it. I got entirely new bills printed for "Lord George Sanger's Circus," and advertised in the newspapers in the same way. Thus everybody began to speak of me as "Lord George," and I became a self-made peer as well as a self-made man.

That is how I became Lord George Sanger to the public. I had been styled "Lord Sanger" when the Burgomaster of Ostend presented me with a gold medal in commemoration of the assistance I was able to give to the poor of Belgium in a terrible flood year, but I never thought of annexing the title till my little legal battle with the Hon. W. Cody. From an advertising point of view it was one of the best things I ever did, and I have often overheard, to my great amusement, very animated discussions as to whether I was really a peer of the realm or not. Now you know the truth, and having told it I hope I may be forgiven if I hang on to the title for the few remaining years that may be left me.

As regards myself and American showmen, I should like to say that outside business rivalries we have always been the best of friends, and my name is as well known in America as it is on this side of the water. At the same time I must insist upon the fact that England has nothing to learn from America, at least as regards the show business. There is nothing that American showmen have ever done that Englishmen have not done first and done better.

In 1860 I gave the first complete hippodrome performance ever witnessed, on the Hoe at Plymouth. I collected about a hundred of the smaller showmen to make a fair, giving them their standings free. Then I had three circus rings and two platforms going at the same time, with a gate admission to the whole show. Twenty-seven years later Barnum and Bailey brought this kind of show to Olympia as a novelty.

In 1874 I made and sold to Mr. P. T. Barnum for £25,000 all the plant for producing "The Congress of Monarchs" in America, as I had produced it at the Agricultural Hall. I had previously sold the right to use my name in America to Messrs. Howe & Co. for £2,000 a year. When Barnum & Co. bought the Howe establishment, they used my name for twelve years as Barnum and Sanger, for which I never received anything. When they came to Olympia it was Barnum and Bailey, my name being dropped because no payments had been made to me. I consulted my solicitors on the matter, but was advised to let it go. I mention these things just to show that in the matter of exhibitions, in spite of tall talk, America has always followed, but never led, the Old Country.

At Bedford, at the time of the Transvaal War, the Americans tried to squeeze me out by slipping into the town when they knew I was going there, and paying an extra sum of money to take the ground I had occupied for many seasons previously. I answered this move by securing a piece of ground at the other end of the town. Then I sent to London and got five thousand torches and a wickerwork figure of Kruger. This ready, I announced a patriotic bonfire and a grand torchlight procession, with torches for all comers. The result was that after the burning of Kruger's effigy and the procession my circus was packed, while the Americans did not take a single shilling. As I said before, they can't hustle the Old Country in the show business.

# CHAPTER XXXIX

## THE WILD WOLVES THAT TERRIFIED LONDON

I USED to play eight and a half months upon the Continent, while running as well a big show on the road in England, and during the winter season would bring part of my plant from abroad to make up my big exhibitions at the theatre in the Westminster Bridge Road and the Agricultural Hall.

One special home-coming I made, and that was for the purpose of arranging and carrying out the procession of Lord Mayor Nottage. This, admittedly one of the finest Lord Mayor's processions ever seen, introduced most of the illustrious personages of history from the time of William the Conqueror downwards. Carriages were specially made for each group; so, too, was the chain and plate armour, for which alone I paid Kennedy, of Birmingham, £2,100. Queen Elizabeth was impersonated by a very handsome lady who came to me, asked for the position without pay, and, looking every inch the part, got it. She used to come to rehearsals, etc., in a costly brougham, and was evidently a lady and very wealthy. I never asked her where she lived or who she was, and when the show was over she left a Bank of England note for £50 to be divided amongst the staff of grooms, and I saw her no more.

After this I produced at Astley's the pantomime of *Gulliver's Travels*, the biggest thing ever attempted by any theatrical or circus manager before or since. In the big scene there were on the stage at the time three hundred girls, two hundred men, two hundred children, thirteen elephants, nine camels, and fifty-two horses, in addition to ostriches, emus, pelicans, deer of all kinds, kangaroos, Indian buffaloes, Brahmin bulls, and, to crown the picture, two living lions led by the collar and chain into the centre of the group.

It brought all London to see it. It likewise brought a letter from the Lord Chamberlain, saying he had been asked to interfere, since nothing but a solid masonry foundation could possibly support safely the weight I was placing on the stage in that one scene. I was able, however, to satisfy his lordship that all was right, and the pantomime ran without a hitch or an accident.

When I decided to drop my Continental tours, after eleven years of more or less success, and confine my business to the home country, things were very bad, and I saw that a sensation was needed to attract attention. I arranged to have one of a rather risky character.

At the Zoological Gardens I had established at Margate I had twelve full-grown wolves, all bred at the Hall-by-the-Sea from old animals that had passed away with age and infirmity, and all as tame as dogs. Still they were wolves, the genuine article, and could be trusted to act as such upon occasion. So I advertised them to perform at my London theatre, and in due course the large den containing them was placed by itself in a thirty-horse stable with plenty of centre room for my purpose.

Then I sent for my slaughterman from Margate. When he arrived I said, "Now, Jim, here's a quid for you," at the same time, to his gratified astonishment, handing him a sovereign. When he had done thanking me I said, "Now, Jim, I want you to go into the stable exactly at eleven o'clock to-night, and you will see an old, worn-out cream horse, whose life has become a misery, tied up near the wolves' cage. When the audience have left the theatre, kill him quickly, and leave him where he falls. Be sure you don't say a word to anyone for six months, and I will then give you a tenner."

I had a young man from Margate at this time whose name was Taylor, but who was professionally "Alpine Charlie." He had a very remarkable countenance, deeply sunken eyes, a heavy jaw, and a most determined expression. His voice matched his looks; his whisper would make a giant tremble, and he was to have the credit of capturing the wolves in the little sensation I had arranged.

Mr. Oliver, my agent; Mr. Reeve, my son-in-law; Jim, the slaughterman, whose mouth was closed by visions of the coming tenner; myself, and Mrs. Sanger were the only people in the plot. Mrs. Sanger was certainly nervous, and kept on saying, "Oh, George! I wish it was all over!" "Oh," I said, "my dear, it'll be all over, and all right very soon. Don't worry!"

So, after some supper, I stole out. The theatre was closed, with the watchman, night fireman, property master, and perhaps a dozen of the hands getting a parting drink at the pit bar as I passed unseen to the stable, which had four doors to it. I closed three, knowing my way quite well in the dark, took down the shutters, opened the iron door, went into the den, and drove the wolves, who had been two days without food, loose into the stable. Then I lit up two jets of gas, and there, sure enough, lay the poor old cream-coloured horse. The slaughterman had done his work. Having observed this, and that the wolves were sniffing the dead gee-gee, I went down to the pit bar for a drop of Scotch.

Having drunk it, I said to the others at the bars, "Now, lads, come on! We want to lock up." Of course, all made a move, and as we went up the drive which led into Palace Road, suddenly looking through the large iron-framed window, I said, "There! What's this? Call the fireman and tell him to turn off that gas. Why is it burning there to waste like that?"

Wells, the fireman, at once came along, but no sooner had he got a glimpse through the window than he cried out, "Oh, my God, the wolves are loose! They've killed one of the horses!" With that he ran frantically into the Palace Road, and, meeting the policeman at the gate of the theatre, told him the news, with the result that the constable set off at full speed for Scotland Yard.

Meanwhile my company were full of excitement, and were bustling about after a glance at the hungry wolves tearing at the carcass of the horse, white-faced and full of fear.

"Where is Alpine Charlie?" I shouted. "At the New Inn, I think, sir," was the reply. "Find him, then!" I cried, and off went a whole army of searchers for the Margate-bred Mountaineer, who had his cue as to when he should be discovered.

The searchers ran from public-house to public-house, with the result that those who thronged the bars at once made for the theatre. By this time twenty policemen were guarding every door, stopping all who tried to enter and were not connected with the theatre. Thousands of people gathered in the roadway, stopping all carriage traffic, and all night long Pressmen from the various newspaper and Press agencies besieged the building. The excitement was intense. I had achieved my sensation!

Next day the papers, not only in London and the provinces, but all over Europe, were full of it. They were quite wolf-struck. The Lord Chamberlain and the wise men of Parliament swallowed the bait, and the Prime Minister was asked if he was aware that "Wolves had broken loose in London, killed a horse, and jeopardized the Queen's subjects?" The Prime Minister was aware. He had heard of the occurrence, and that the wolves had been safely caged again by a plucky performer at the circus named Alpine Charlie. What he did not know, and what he was not likely to learn, was that the terrible animals had slunk without protest into their den when Charlie, with a rattan cane, had appeared amongst them and said,

"Get in there!" Even Prime Ministers may miss the inwardness of a prearranged wolf-scare!

The following week the wolves appeared in conjunction with the circus and pantomime, and everybody came to see them and their marvellous tamer, Alpine Charlie. There have been times when I have been quite sad about the deception I practised in connection with those wolves, but a liver pill has invariably restored my equanimity.

# CHAPTER XL

## GOOD-BYE TO ASTLEY'S

AFTER running the great theatre in the Westminster Bridge Road for twenty-two years I resolved to give it up. For some time the Ecclesiastical Commissioners, who were the ground landlords, had been desirous of acquiring the property, and the new authorities in London, full of fads and fancies, had begun to treat me in a manner which the word "unfair" but mildly characterizes.

In 1888 I was called upon by the Metropolitan Board of Works to make extensive alterations, which I did, at a cost of over £6,000. The theatre had not been running more than six weeks when I was summoned before Mr. Biron, at Westminster, for not opening a certain door and supplying it with a spring fastening, so as to render it of easy exit.

Now, that very door had been bricked up outside by order of the Board of Works when the alterations were made. The surveyor, however, a new-comer, who summoned me, anxious to make a show of activity, I suppose, had never troubled to ascertain the facts, but rushed into action at once, after a casual view from inside the building.

When the matter was explained in court Mr. Biron was very sarcastic at the expense of the authorities, and said had he known "the facts of the whole ridiculous business," he should not have granted the summons. I came out with flying colours, and obtained my costs, which, of course, was very well as far as it went; but, at the same time, the matter rankled. It was a sign that officialdom was growing in power, and had every desire to become tyrannous.

The following year the County Council was inaugurated, and, when it got settled down to business, plied the new broom with more zeal than discretion. I had repainted and redecorated throughout, when down came the new inspectors. To them the name of the old Board of Works was simply "anathema." No matter how good anything might be, the fact that it had the sanction of the previous authority was sufficient to damn it in L.C.C. eyes. The consequence was that the whole of the work I had had done, at the cost of so many thousands, was utterly condemned, and I was called upon to practically rebuild the theatre.

As things were shaping, this was more than I could undertake to do, so very reluctantly I took the cheque offered me by the Ecclesiastical Commissioners, and on March 4th, 1893, gave up the key, and surrendered Astley's world-famous amphitheatre to destruction.

My heart was very sore at leaving the place which had witnessed so many of my triumphs, and others sorrowed with me. When I had announced my final performance, and was dismantling the building, prior to giving up possession, artists in the circus profession came from all parts of the country to take a last look at the old ring in which most of them had performed. Two gentlemen, sons of famous riders and trick-act gymnasts, who had acquired wealth, actually made special journeys from America in order to see the last of Astley's and to carry back some mementoes of the magic circle wherein their progenitors had won the plaudits of admiring spectators.

I may as well mention here that it was at the theatre in the Westminster Bridge Road I acquired the King's ring which I possess, and of which so much has been heard in regard to its size, value, and workmanship.

I was exhibiting "The only White Elephant ever seen in the Western World" when I was honoured by a visit from his Majesty, then Prince of Wales. He was very anxious to have a close view of the elephant, a beautiful creature, whose shining milk-white skin made it the admiration of all beholders.

So, after the performance, I conducted the Prince through the stables, and showed him all there was to see. When we came to the "White Elephant" stall, H.R.H. suddenly turned to me and said, "Sanger, is this really one of the sacred white elephants?"

To this I replied, "Well, your Royal Highness, a showman is entitled to practise a little deception on the crowd, but I should never think of deceiving my future King. As you see, it is certainly a 'white' elephant – in fact, a very white elephant, but only because we give him a coat of special whitewash twice a day!"

My goodness, how the Prince did laugh! He thought the "white elephant" a splendid joke, more especially when I told him that I was once offered the genuine article, but refused the animal as useless for showing as a "white" elephant. It was a patchwork-looking beast, whose nearest approach to white consisted in having various large pinky blotches on its body. There was no doubt about its pedigree, or that it was one of the true Siamese sacred and so-called "white" elephants. But it was not white. The people wanted a white elephant, so I let the Siamese beast go, and, assisting nature with art, gave them what they desired – a handsome creature white as driven snow. The Prince, now our gracious King, kept his counsel regarding the elephant, and later sent me the ring I so treasure, a jewel he obtained when on his Indian tour. It is unique in design, forming a heavy gold strap that buckle about the finger, and is set with seven large diamonds in the strap and 365 small brilliants round the buckle. Truly a kingly present.

While I proudly mention the many triumphs I secured at Astley's, I must incidentally remark that spectacular success did not always mean profits in proportion. For instance, in the spectacle of "The Fall of Khartoum and Death of General Gordon" that I produced there for two hundred and eighty consecutive performances, I put on nightly three hundred men of the Guards, four hundred supers, one hundred camels, two hundred real Arab horses, the fifes and drums of the Grenadiers, and the pipers of the Scots Guards. It drew tremendous houses, and made a fine advertisement for my travelling circus, but all the same I made a loss by it of just over £10,000.

So, too, in regard to the menagerie which was such a feature of my show. The expense was tremendous. Wild animals are, any of them, most delicate creatures costing hundreds of pounds to buy, and then pining away and dying, despite all the care and kindness that may be lavished upon them.

As an item in this direction I may mention that I once bought from the late Mr. Jamrach, the world-famous East End animal dealer, six young giraffes he had managed to get to London alive. I paid him £1,200 cash down for them, and he undertook to keep them on his premises for a few days until I could fetch them away. Three days later, when I called on him, two of the giraffes were dead, and before I could remove them the four others died also. It was no fault of Mr. Jamrach's, who very generously gave me back £300 of the money I had paid him over my unfortunate deal; it was just the luck that attaches to animal buying. When the beasts are safely in your care, if you want to keep them in condition there must be no relaxation of attention either by night or by day. This often means much personal worry and loss of rest. As an example of this I may mention that I once sat up two days and two nights with a sick lion, and managed to save his life by putting mustard plasters on his chest.

It was the big lion who used to ride in the circus procession on the top of the car with the lamb. He was a powerful but kindly tempered beast, and when after catching a bad cold it developed pneumonia it nearly broke my heart to see him suffer.

I resolved to save him if I could, so I went into the den with him and, sending for packet after packet of mustard, got it mixed and then rubbed it through his thick fur well into his chest and round his sides. This was an all-night job, and the poor old fellow, who seemed to know it was for his good, never made the slightest resistance.

At last I got the mustard well caked in a plaster round the lion; then I had him littered up with straw, so as to practically cover him. Under the wagon which held him coke fires were lit, so that the warmth should strike up through the boards. Then, feeling I had done my best, I sat down to watch the patient. In twenty-four hours he was vastly improved, and in a week was convalescent. Twelve months later I sold him in the very pink of health and condition to the Barnum combination, and he made a big sensation in America. Such are some of the incidents that befall those who make wild beasts their care.

# CHAPTER XLI

## MEETING WITH ROYALTY AND A GRACIOUS QUEEN'S LETTER

Now I must hurry on and bring my story to a close, for I feel that the latter days of my career, however important they may be to myself, have not the interest for my readers that attaches to the earlier period.

Well, after giving up the theatre in the Westminster Bridge Road, I paid close attention to my great travelling circus and my establishments at Margate and Ramsgate. At the latter place I may mention I had purchased from the corporation a considerable portion of the High Street, and erected there an amphitheatre, an hotel, and various shops, at a cost of something like £60,000. I still hold it, and though I have gone out of the travelling circus business, hope to entertain the public there, and at the Hall-by-the-Sea, Margate, till the time comes for me to depart altogether from this world.

That, however, is by the way. Now to get on with my tale.

After leaving Astley's I took my circus everywhere. From Land's End to John o' Groats all the folks knew and welcomed "Lord" George Sanger and his establishment. Features of my entertainment were the big military spectacles, in which were reproduced as faithfully as possible dramatic incidents of real warfare.

One of my last ventures, when Africa was so much in the popular mind, was to try to prove that ostrich farming could be carried on here as successfully as it is on that vast continent. Anyhow, I knew it would provide an interesting feature, so I purchased twenty-five ostriches, at a cost of £30 each, from Mr. Carl Hagenbeck, and carried them with me about the country.

If the birds did not encourage the idea of farming them here, as I had hoped they would do, they looked very nice in their great glass car in the procession, and kept the audience at night highly excited and amused when they were introduced into a spectacular ostrich hunt.

There was only one untoward incident in connection with them, and that occurred at Bedford. Hard by the circus ground – a fine green expanse – ran the river, and on its banks in the early morning we used to let the big birds have a run to stretch their legs. One morning they got too much of a run. The local foxhounds came that way, and in a moment the dogs, barking with excitement, were after the ostriches. The latter, frightened out of the few senses they possess, got into the river out of the way of the hounds. While the huntsman was taking the latter off I and my staff had a lively time trying to save the ostriches from drowning. We got them all safely out of the river at last, and they proved to be none the worse for their adventure. But it might very well have been disastrous to the birds, and, at any rate, the incident convinced me that foxhounds, ostriches and a handy river on a chilly morning constitute, from the circus proprietor's point of view, anything but a desirable combination.

Every year after giving up the Westminster Bridge Road Theatre I made it a point to tour with my circus in Scotland, where I always had a great reception and did splendid business.

It was on one of these tours, in 1893, that I had the honour of appearing before the Duke and Duchess of Fife. They came to see my circus, and brought all their household with them, and afterwards I was invited to a special audience at Duff House.

I shall never forget my kindly reception, from which all formality was absent. I saw the Duke and her Royal Highness the Duchess together; the latter, who has all the urbanity of her Royal father, King Edward, was nursing her baby, the Lady Maud, who had been born the previous April.

The Duchess put some very shrewd questions to me, showing that she had a remarkable grasp of business matters. Her Royal Highness was especially anxious to know if I had much trouble in managing my big establishment, with its hundreds of employees, and took much interest in the details I gave her. I was royally entertained before leaving, and received a memento of the visit in the shape of the head of a magnificent horned sheep, mounted in silver-gilt with crystals and cairngorms, and so prepared as to form a combination of snuff mull and a cigar and cigarette cabinet. It is one of my most treasured ornaments.

When in Scotland I on several occasions desired to give a performance before Queen Victoria, but until 1898 something always happened to prevent it. In June that year my circus was at

Ballater, and I had a handsome pair of Shetland ponies that I hoped her Majesty would accept as a present. However, the command did not come, and I had to go off to do some pressing business in London, leaving my manager in charge. He had not long got away from Ballater when the command came that the Queen desired to witness the circus.

Back he went, of course, at once, and on Friday, June 19th, 1898, the performance was given at Balmoral, and the Queen graciously accepted the ponies the manager presented in my name. I was dreadfully disappointed at not being present, but as soon as I was apprised of the command I sent a loyal telegram of thanks to her Majesty for her kindness in honouring me.

In response I received a most delightful letter from Balmoral, signed by Sir Arthur Bigge, the Queen's Private Secretary, in which he conveyed her Majesty's thanks for the ponies, and then went on to say:–

The Queen was very sorry that owing to a mistake application for the circus to come here was not made until it had left Ballater, which her Majesty fears must have entailed much extra trouble and fatigue. I have further to express the thanks of the Queen for the kindly and loyal sentiments contained in your telegram I am forwarding to Mrs Sanger from the Queen a small souvenir of Friday's performance, which her Majesty witnessed with much interest and satisfaction.

That was a beautiful letter, and it filled me with pride and gratitude, while my dear wife was overwhelmed with delight at her present, which consisted of a splendid bracelet.

I little thought at that period of happiness how short a time would be hers to enjoy its possession, and that I was nearing my life's greatest calamity. I have been thankful since that no premonition occurred to darken those pleasant days; that a merciful Providence allows us to enjoy ourselves while we may by giving us no foreknowledge of the future.

# CHAPTER XLII

## THE LATTER YEARS, SOME PARTINGS, AND FAREWELL

ON the last day of April, 1899, I was stricken by the heaviest blow I ever received. My dear wife, who had been ailing for some two months, died with unexpected suddenness. Only those who have undergone such a loss will be able to understand my overwhelming grief.

For over forty-eight years she had been the constant partner of my joys and sorrows, and in all that time no single word of anger or fault-finding had occurred between us. Always ready to help me with advice, and that advice always sound and useful, never once did she question any decision I had arrived at, but always strove to help me carry out my purposes. We were lovers to the last, and when I laid her in the family tomb at Margate I felt as though the light of my life was quenched for ever.

It is a subject I do not care to dwell upon, though time has softened the first sharpness of the sorrow that is mine in losing such a partner.

For weeks I felt dazed and helpless. Work I knew to be the best panacea for my pain, but business had lost its interest for me. I wanted something to rouse me, and that something came to me at last at the hand of that ever gracious and kindly lady, our lamented Queen Victoria.

On June 9th, 1899, I received a letter from Balmoral from Sir Arthur Bigge, informing me that the Queen would like to see my procession and circus when I came into the neighbourhood of Windsor. To that, of course, I at once replied that I would be ready at Windsor on any date that it might please her Majesty to fix. Another letter, dated June 21st, came in reply to this, stating that the Queen would like to witness the circus procession at a quarter to five on the afternoon of Monday, July 17th.

So on the great day I went to Windsor, and in the courtyard of the Castle paraded my show, with every adjunct and embellishment I could think of, before the Sovereign I had so often longed to see and have speech with.

The Queen watched the spectacle from her carriage, and liked it so well that she had the parade repeated. When it was over Sir Arthur Bigge came to me and said that her Majesty desired that I should be presented to her. Then he led me to the Royal carriage, and as I bowed low, said, "Your Majesty, this is Mr. Sanger."

Never, if I live to be a thousand years old, could I forget that interview. As I straightened myself from another bow I saw the eyes of my Sovereign upon me, the gaze full of kindness.

In a voice singularly high, clear and penetrating, the Queen said, "So you are Mr. Sanger?" "Yes, your Majesty," I replied.

Then, with a smile and a twinkle in those steadfast eyes, "*Lord* George Sanger, I believe?"

This, with the accent on the "Lord," was distinctly embarrassing, but I managed to stammer out," Yes, if your Majesty pleases!"

"It is very amusing," was the Royal lady's answer, "and I gather you have borne the title very honourably!"

"Thank you, your Majesty," I said; "your gracious kindness overwhelms me!"

"Do you know, you seem very young, Mr. Sanger?"

"Yes, your Majesty," said I; "but it may surprise you to hear that it was on the day of your Majesty's Coronation, at the fair in Hyde Park, that I put on my first performing dress!"

The Queen expressed her astonishment at this, and then I had to answer a whole fire of questions about my circus and the animals, particularly the elephants, in which her Majesty took a great interest. Some touching words of sympathy with me in my recent great bereavement followed, and the interview, which had lasted nearly ten minutes – an unusually long time I was afterwards informed – was over.

As she went away the Queen called out, "Sir Arthur, be sure you remunerate Mr. Sanger!" and then the most gracious of gracious ladies was driven rapidly towards the Castle.

Immediately afterwards Sir Arthur Bigge asked me to accompany him to his official room, and when we got there was about to write out a cheque. I at once stopped him, and said that any insistence on my receiving monetary remuneration would make me very unhappy. So he shut up his cheque book with the remark, "Very well, Sanger, then we must find you a souvenir."

A few days later I received a massive silver cigar-box, on the lid of which was engraved:–

Mr. George Sanger.
V.R.I.
Windsor Castle, July 17th, 1899.

I was the last entertainer to receive a present from Queen Victoria, and I value the splendid gift accordingly.

Though I never saw our noble Queen again, yet I was shortly to be reminded that the interest she evinced in me and my animals was altogether unfeigned.

This reminder came over the unfortunate incident at the Crystal Palace in the following February, when my elephant "Charlie" killed a man who had teased him beyond endurance.

The story is briefly this: some grooms and a carpenter connected with my menagerie, then at the Palace, had been to the big hotel near the entrance on a Sunday, and there bragged to some friends what they could do with the animals, and particularly the elephants.

The carpenter and another man took their friends into the Palace to display their prowess over the great beasts, and roused them to fury by prodding them with some lances used by my company in the spectacle of the Soudan War.

"Charlie" came in for several nasty pricks, and at length broke his leg chain in his rage and went for the carpenter, who had been his principal assailant. The elephant knocked the unfortunate man down, then crushed him to death with his head, and finished by seizing the body with his trunk and dashing it repeatedly on the ground till it lost all semblance of humanity.

During the scene the other elephants, mad with excitement, broke loose, and the great tusker, "Edgar," rushed trumpeting into the concert hall, where a Sunday concert was proceeding. He then made his way into the open, and was away for two nights and a day, doing all sorts of damage before he was captured.

I was at once sent for, and by the aid of another elephant, "Mary," whom at the risk of my life I led up to the furious "Charlie," and attached to the mad beast's broken leg chain by a neck rope, I got the great creature to a stout pillar, and there securely fastened him.

Then I wired to a Strand gunmaker, who sent down three men with elephant guns, and on my directions they killed the poor beast with a single volley.

At the inquest on the carpenter it was clearly shown that the man had brought his death upon himself by teasing the elephant, and I was congratulated by the coroner and the jury on the part I had played in securing and killing the creature before further damage resulted.

I did not congratulate myself, I can tell you, for I had had poor Charlie twenty years, and was very fond of him. In the ordinary way I could do anything with him, and had once relieved him of a loose and aching tooth, an act for which he showed his satisfaction by giving me, whenever I came near him, a gentle hug with his trunk.

In the course of my career I have lost thirteen elephants, "Charlie" being the last and most mourned. "Edgar" was secured after he had tired himself out, and was brought back in quite a subdued frame of mind. What I paid to make good the damage he did and the loss of "Charlie" totalled up to close upon £3,000. That was indeed a black Sunday for me.

The one piece of gratification in the affair was the interest shown by the Queen. Directly following the occurrence I got the letter from Windsor Castle, dated February 21st, 1900, which was reproduced earlier in my story, expressing the desire of her Majesty to know all the particulars, and asking as to the identity of the elephants concerned. An answer was, of course, promptly sent, and then came another letter from Windsor from Sir Arthur Bigge, dated February 24th, 1900, as follows:–

DEAR MR. SANGER

The Queen desires me to thank you for replying to her inquiries about the unfortunate occurrence with the elephants. The evidence at the inquest made one sad for evidently poor "Charlie" had been goaded into his dangerous condition. The Queen also wishes me to thank you for the photograph of yourself, and also of those scenes taken here in which figure both "Charlie" and "Archie."

"Archie" was an elephant that appeared at Windsor.

Could there ever have been kinder communications between Sovereign and subject than these? I doubt it, and my mind is full of gratitude to that noble Queen who so honoured me, and to whose glorious memory it has been my privilege to be allowed to erect a humble tribute in the marketplace of my native town of Newbury.

Now I feel that I must bring my story to an end. It has already exceeded the dimensions I originally planned for it, and further talk of my triumphs as a showman between the death of Queen

Victoria and my retirement in 1905 might savour of vainglory, and would only tire those who have patiently borne with me thus far.

There are some things, too, that though they may be worth mention are not good to dwell upon at any length. Such, for instance, was my venture in the promoting line, when for a time my circus became a limited company. I had been ill, and the magnitude of my business pressed heavily upon me. So when certain persons came to me and painted the possibilities of an easier life with a flourishing company if I could consent to let them arrange matters, I foolishly yielded.

The result was that I added a hundredfold to my responsibilities, and was nearly worried into my grave. As the judge in an action that arose over the scheme pointed out, all the money that was found for the company came out of my pocket, while others reaped a harvest over the sale of shares. In the end, in order to maintain my name for honesty and fair dealing, and so that innocent people who had been deluded by false promises might not suffer, I paid them out at a loss of £40,000, got my circus back into my own hands, and once more made a big success of it. That is all that need be said of that episode.

It was in these latter days – in fact, in March, 1903 – that the Prince of Wales honoured me with his command, and I venture to think that the exhibition I gave lacked none of its former glories. At any rate, the Prince was so pleased that he gave me a magnificent and appropriately inscribed silver grace cup, to take pride of place among my other trophies.

Two years later I concluded that the time had arrived for me to retire from the road. I was still active, hale and hearty, but I was past the allotted span of life, and thought it best to seek rest while men still spoke well of me.

Accordingly, on Tuesday and Wednesday, October 31st and November 1st, 1905, I disposed of all my circus appliances, horses, and wild animals – everything except my own old living-wagon – in a great two days' sale at my farm at East Finchley. I let them go when times were good, for I had had the best tenting season I had known for six years when the hammer fell upon the lots. From March 21st to October 21st, 1905, I had travelled 3,300 miles, with a record journey of 74½ miles, and two performances in twenty-four hours. I think that was an excellent finish for a man who had been on the road for three score years and ten.

When our last performance had been given, all my company,

from the highest to the lowest – most of them with the tears running down their cheeks formed up in a circle, and sang "Auld Lang Syne." That was the end of Lord George Sanger's great English circus.

This year I have severed my connections with the Showman's Guild that I established eighteen years ago. It can run without me now, and I drop the president's mallet, not without regret, but rejoicing that the showmen are at last united to secure their best interests in a strong society.

I have still my theatres at Ramsgate and Margate, so I am not cut quite away from old associations, but shall remain a showman to the end of my days. What those days have been I have striven to tell you to the best of my ability, and if I have only brought to you something of the glamour and romance which teem for me in recalling them my labour has not been in vain.

For me there remains now only their "memories" – memories that fill me with a glad thankfulness as I contrast the past days with the present ones. Yet, like Lindsay Gordon's "Stockman," were the choice given me, "I should live the same life over if I had to live again," rejoicing in the strenuous days of the open road, whose song is for ever ringing in my ears.

And now – Farewell! God bless you all, my friends, wherever you may be. Good roads, good times and merry tenting! That is the showman's benison!

# SANGER AND HIS TIMES by Kenneth Grahame

RETIREMENT and reminiscence are apt to trot in harness together, and so, when Mr. George Sanger, the great showman, so familiar, by name at least, to the youth of the last generation, retired from the circus business in 1905, he proceeded to set down the simple yet moving annals of his past career, with the same calm courage with which he would draw the aching tooth of a favourite elephant. Published in book form in 1910, under the title of *Seventy Years a Showman*, these memoirs hardly attracted at the time all the notice they really merited. It is to be hoped that this re-issue – the book has been many years out of print – may receive fuller attention, for his story is not only excellently and graphically written, and packed with yarns of the most vivid character set forth in a perfectly natural and unexaggerated manner, but it provides a reel, so to speak, of moving-pictures illustrative of a certain period – that extending from the early thirties to the end of the last century – during which the rural and provincial life of England underwent a transformation as complete as perhaps any previous period of seventy years could show. It covers, too, the whole period of Dickens's work, and that of many another of lesser fame, all busy depicting the Early Victorian world in its every phase; and once more, as we read, many of their characters seem to start into life again, each in his habit as he lived, in the faithful jottings of this simple and unlettered showman.

George Sanger's parents were Wiltshire people; his father, "press-ganged" at eighteen, served ten years afloat, and fought (and was severely wounded) in the *Victory* at Trafalgar; from which event, and his consequent retirement on a pension of £10 per annum, we date his entry into the show business, with a self-made peep-show he could carry on his back. As described by his son, he seems to have been a man of fine character, and his adventures, intertwined as they are with the writer's early years, form as good reading as any part of the book. But the father, though reaching out at times in this direction and that, remained faithful in the main to the peep-show with which he had first challenged fortune. It was young George who was always the climber, the aspirant, the seeker after new things. While still a boy, he must needs start his own little show, which, composed of performing canaries, redpolls and white mice, strengthened later by two tame hares, bore in it the seed of the mighty circuses and menageries that were to follow. At eighteen he was on the road with a travelling van of his own; when about twenty-six he entered the great circusworld, and passed from success to success, their culmination being the purchase of the famous Astley's Theatre in 1871. Followed his Continental tours and triumphs, during which, as he used to boast, his circuses travelled the roads of every country in Europe except Russia; and thereafter he was not so much a man as an institution – and a British institution too.

Mr. Sanger, like a good showman, married in the profession, choosing for his bride the popular Lion Queen of a rival establishment, somewhat to the disgust of the rival establishment, who evidently held, not unnaturally, that showmen ought to marry their own Lion Queens, instead of poaching on those of other people. She made as good a wife as she had made a Lion Queen – who dares to say that an early training is ever entirely wasted? – and when, after forty-eight years of happy married life, he lost her, his book pays touching tribute to all that she had been to him, both in solid worth and in affection. "Lovers to the last," he says – and that is saying not a little.

In 1905 Mr. Sanger, finding himself approaching his eightieth year, sold up all his circuses and animals, and finally retired from active business, settling down on his farm at East Finchley; and there it might have been expected he would end his days peacefully, looking back, in his well-earned repose, on many golden memories of past struggles and successes. Fate ordered otherwise. Many will remember the tragedy. In 1911 a manservant in his employ, of a sullen and revengeful disposition, fired by some real or fancied grievance over which he had probably brooded long, suddenly ran amok, as it were, attacked two fellow-men-servants, wounding one of them severely, and battered the life out of poor old Mr. Sanger with a hatchet.

In so piteous a fashion passed away the famous old showman, the gallant and kindly of spirit, the friend and benefactor of all poor travelling show-people, the founder of the Showmen's Guild, the author of an autobiography which contains not an unkind word of anybody.

As to shows themselves, the townsman does not quite realize all the signs and tokens by which the country-dweller knows that the year has really turned, that spring has thrown out its advancing pickets, and that the main forces of summer are well on their way. He knows, indeed, that we hail, each in their turn, the thrust of the snowdrop and then the crocus, the first green thrill that passes over the quickset hedgerows, the tender wash of faint water-colour that tells of the winter wheat now thrusting through, the touch of rosiness in the black elm tree-tops; but perhaps he does not know that one of the truest signs of approaching summer to us is when a sort of frozen Neva in his own suburbs thaws and breaks up, and the flood of caravans that have been winter-bound there is let loose at last – caravans that are to make the little village fairs of the countryside; simple little fairs that nevertheless mean so very much to us.

In a hedgeless country of high downland, on a road that came flowing down, a long white ribbon, straight as it were out of the eastern sky, we would watch, each succeeding spring, for the first appearance of these fairy cruisers of the road. Of course the earliest comers were not for us humble villagers. These would "open" at the larger provincial towns, and then start on the circuit they had each planned out for themselves, and we should have to wait our turn, having a couple of nights thrown to us, or perhaps three, if the dates in *Old Moore's Almanac* allowed of it. ("Old Moore" is the *locus classicus* for the dates of country fairs, so most farmers keep it on their mantelpiece.) But when at last we caught sight of a certain small yellow caravan, with pretty Mrs. S. and the latest baby sitting in front, her husband (who had charge of the dart throwing department) walking at the horse's head, then we knew that our turn had come at last! "Enter Autolycus singing!" For close on the yellow caravan would surely come the larger one, with father and mother and the cooking utensils; and then that other which held Mrs. S.'s three comely young sisters, whom we knew as the Princesses, each, though so young, already a specialist of some sort, and who all slept in one broad bed placed across the rear of their caravan, looking, I should imagine, like three little St. Ursulas by Carpaccio. Later the swing-boats and the wooden horses would straggle in, and all the paraphernalia of the stalls and booths, and the horses (not the wooden ones, of course) would be led away and picketed. Then perhaps, beside a late camp fire, time would be found to renew acquaintance and hear all the news of the past winter; for the winters, to the women at least, were by no means a period of suspended animation.

One does not, it seems, when autumn is over, desert one's caravan for humdrum bricks and mortar. One camps, by arrangement with someone or other, on some piece of waste land or only partly used builder's yard or undeveloped building site on the outskirts of London itself, or of the big new towns, but lately villages themselves, that have sprung up as dormitories to the great city; and there, through all weathers, through rain and frost and snow, one sticks it out in one's little wooden caravan. This may sound very poor fun; but the actual fact was far otherwise. These girls were at first quite strangely reluctant to enlarge upon the joys of a leisured winter life in the neighbourhood of a large city. The reason for this only transpired later, and showed a quite charming delicacy of feeling on their part. "We thought," they explained in effect," that it would make you dissatisfied with your hard lot as compared with ours, and perhaps you would be feeling jealous and discontented. For you live in this poky remote little village all the year round, and see nothing and know nothing, and never even guess at all the glamour and excitement that more fortunately placed classes such as ours are free to enjoy." We meekly admitted our social disadvantages, but pressed to be allowed a peep at urban life and its glories; and by degrees heard all about the jolly excursions to town, after the train with the black-coated city men had departed, the visits to Parks, Piccadillies, Regent Streets; the studies of shop-windows, and all the ladies' frocks; then bun-shops, matinees, more bun-shops, and a first-class performance at some West End theatre; finally the rush for the last train back, the sleepy journey down, the tramp along a muddy lane and across a field or two to the little caravan at last, making a blacker spot against the dull winter sky; and then the cheerful dazzle of the reflector-lamp on the wall, the cup of cocoa and snack of supper, and laughter and sense of snugness; and so to bed at last, St. Ursula-wise, in the little cabin that was all their very own.

Indeed, the show-people are a contented folk, chiefly, I think, because they rarely want to be anything but what they are. They like the life for itself, not for its gains and profits. They generally seem to have enough money, if not a great superfluity. Some people seem to have a vague idea of travelling show-folk as living in Rembrandt interiors on a Salvator Rosa background, in a scene of perpetual high lights and fuliginous shadows full of flashing eyes, tangled gipsy locks, dirt, confusion, clamour and picturesqueness. They are instead a quiet and reserved people, subdued in manner, clannish, living a life apart; scrupulously clean and tidy, as indeed anyone must be who lives in a caravan; self-reliant, asking little from anyone except some tolerance from officials and freedom to come and go and offer their simple wares; and you rarely find a gipsy among them. They intermarry among themselves, and are very proud of their descent from some bygone Champion Sword-swallower or Queen of the Tight-rope; success, if it comes to them, is but modest, reckoned in terms of money; failure means that they are down and out, and there will be no one waiting to help them, except perhaps their own folk.

I have said they are a contented people, and so they are, especially the elders. But among the younger ones, as is natural enough, a little breeze blowing from the land of What-might-have-been will sometimes stir and rustle the leaves of contemplative thought. The Princesses told us they had another married sister, and that *she* lived in a house with a real doorstep, which she could whiten, twice a day if she liked! "But," we protested, "look at the beautiful steps of your own caravan! Real mahogany, with brass finishings, and hook off and on with a touch!" "Yes, but you can't *whiten* them," sighed the Princesses wistfully. "And, besides," they added, "*she* has a permanent address!" They went on to confess that when the time came for them to think of marriage too, they intended to aim high – to aim even at a permanent address and a doorstep that could be whitened! Such are the rash dreams of youth! But it is good to carry an ideal about with you, however unattainable it be; and, as R. L. Stevenson has it, to travel hopefully (and in a caravan too!) is better than to arrive (even at a whiteable doorstep).

These girls, by the way, wore the long, tightwaisted corsets in which the fisher-girls, and factory girls too, of Boulogne so delight the eye. And within the last few weeks I have encountered young gipsy women on the road in just the same type of corset. It was a real pleasure to see it again, with its touch of old-worldliness and even of dignity. If a Paris dressmaker can be imagined visiting a Berkshire common, she might be tempted to try a revision of next season's fashions, and give us an outline once more – if it was only, like Mr. Mantalini's dowager's, a demd outline.

Talking of caravan steps, which are really short ladders, almost perpendicular and without handrail, these have a special influence on the development of the caravan child. For the caravan-born infant, as soon as it can notice anything at all, is swift to detect the contrast between his own cabin'd, cribb'd, confined surroundings and the wonderful great world he catches a glimpse of through the little door – a world consisting of a mighty green common, dotted with white geese plucking at the grass of it, and horses and donkeys tethered here and there, and Daddy and other gods passing freely to and fro. But alas! between you and it stretches a mighty cliff, down which a dizzy ladder crawls! Well, what of it? Such things have got to be tackled sooner or later. So as soon as it can roll or wriggle, and certainly before it can walk, the caravan-infant is down that ladder, somehow, and in due course up it again, and no one knows how it does it, because they are too busy to notice, and they wouldn't interfere if they did in any case, and it never falls, and wouldn't in the least mind if it did. Few things, I think, are more permanent than the amusements that go to make up a country fair. Changes, of course, come along in time, but they are slow, and more in the nature of adaptations and improvements than revolutions. I suppose the most eternal feature of a fair is the Roundabout. As the highest expression of the emotion of joy, we would all of us naturally choose to spring upon a charger and ride forth at top speed into the boundless prairie. As we can hardly do that and yet be back in time for tea; we go round and round and shut our eyes at intervals, trying to imagine that we are travelling as straight as a cannon-ball. And if the horse must needs be of wood, at least it is steady and demands small skill from its rider. I will here ask connoisseurs of this form of *haute ecole* to note that in the best circles such horses have their names painted on their necks, and that these names are never invented; they are all the names of very real horses of old time, taken from some official studbook or other. This ought to add an interest to every ride, in a real sportsman. Once I had the fortune to bestride the mighty Eclipse himself, in wooden effigy; and what gave that ride its special touch of romance was, that it was in a small provincial town but a few miles from the very place where that peerless horse was foaled. Only a day or two before I had walked over the now desolate spot on the edge of the downs. Wheeled over by plover and played upon by rabbits, only some slight irregularities of the turf that now covered the site told where once a great house stood.

The English public is faithful in the main to horses, and does not greatly care to ride a bear or an ostrich. Pink pigs with blue ribbons round their necks, so popular in France, where the whole roundabout will consist of placid pink pigs, I have never met in

England, though there are few more pleasing sights than M. le Maire, M. le Notaire, and the rest of the principal inhabitants of a small French town, clad in straw hats, long black frock-coats, and yellow boots well turned up at the toes, gravely circling round, each on the back of the pinkest and shiniest of pigs. The great farmyard cock, again, crested and open-beaked, with wings outstretched and one brawny, scaly leg flung far behind him, is not so usual as in France – which perhaps is natural. It is the old English instinct to bestride a horse and not a griffin.

But horses must give way, in shows as elsewhere, to the march of time, and dummy motor-cars have long challenged the supremacy of Eclipse and his mates. Children, I think, prefer them, because they can grasp the dummy steering-wheel and pretend they are driving. And pretend they do, most earnestly. And now to the cars has succeeded a new thing, the chairoplane, which assuredly has come to stay. This fairy thing, with its birdlike undulations, its rushes and its tarryings, is as attractive to look upon as (I should imagine) to form a part of. It is a pretty sight, on some ancient village green, while the upper sky still holds the waning daylight, and the flares are lighting up over the ground below, to see a dozen village maidens, with the silk stockings, scanty skirts and shingled heads that were denied their less emancipated mothers of my own youth, flying with the motion of doves far above one's head. As the poet has it,

Although I enter not,
Yet round about the spot
Oft-times I hover!

As one stands at gaze the daylight slowly wanes, the yellower flares begin to take charge of the atmosphere, the organ brays and the speed increases, and the fluttering riders swing out horizontally in the most bewitching of poses; then sink languidly, droopingly, to rest and earth, and the spell is broken.

Next to the roundabouts must surely be ranked the swing-boats, that tear the insides out of you at the top of every ascent; beloved of the younger and more daring sort, because there seems always just a ghost of a chance that by an extra hard pull one may succeed in completing the revolution and looping the loop. And then we come to another class of sport altogether, the coco-nut throwing, ring-throwing, dart-throwing, all for some very small chance of winning a prize. (Coco-nuts, be it noted, were too expensive to be given away in the young Sanger's days.) Some joy in one's skill as a Discobolus may enter into these sports, but the real inspiring motive is the gambler's. Indeed these poor little wooings of fortune may be said to have atrophied down from the full-blooded days when fairs, and especially racecourses, had their gambling booths open to all and free of interference, each with its tempting piles of gold and silver displayed on its long table. To sum up, then, it may be roughly said that the joys of a fair range themselves under two heads – the delight of exhilarating motion; the excitement of an element of gamble, however trumpery the possible reward.

Perhaps the greatest change that has taken place in show-life in our generation is the disappearance of freaks and monstrosities; and this, it will surely be agreed by all, is a change entirely for good. Of old, freaks were the mainstay of every show. The first pair of importance that I ever attended – I was ten years old at the time – was that of St. Giles's, at Oxford, and I seem to recollect that giants, dwarfs, fat ladies, tattooed ladies, mermaids, six-legged calves and distorted nature of every variety formed the backbone of the show. These have now passed away, and the public taste no longer demands to be disgusted. It must be twenty years since I saw even so much as a fat lady, and that was far down in the West Country, where traditions linger and preferences die hard. Although a printed notice informed you that this mountain of flesh was so genuine throughout that any lady in the audience was permitted, nay invited, to test by pinching, though gentlemen, in the interest of good manners, were kindly requested to refrain; and though a biographical pamphlet related, *inter alia*, that Madame Aurelia's bulk entirely forbade her travelling by train, and a special two-horse van had therefore to be kept at her disposal, yet one could not help feeling uneasily, as one gazed in awe, that there was something wanting. A day or two later, having taken my place in a third-class compartment of a local train, I was greatly pleased when Madame Aurelia – in mufti of course – hopped in as lightly as a bird. We were already five a side, but Madame Aurelia's arrival did not seem to affect our density particularly. She was an amusing woman, and was the life and soul (if hardly the body) of the company, who could not know of course – for there was really nothing to tell them – that they were entertaining such an angel unawares. Illusion, as the showman knows, is nearly everything.

But I have sometimes reflected since, that my cheerful

acquaintance of the railway carriage had possibly been understudying the real Madame Aurelia, and that on that occasion we had all been "spoofed". Verily the showman hath need of "spoof" as well as illusion. As in the famous picture of Garrick between Tragedy and Comedy, the showman walks between Spoof and Illusion, hand in hand with both. Yet freaks may still linger on, here and there; but I have not seen a real freak-collection since the days of Barnum, who rather specialized in freaks and always put them in the forefront of his shows. But Barnum, though a great showman, was a bit behind the times, on this side of the water at least. Freaks were already becoming *démodés* when he brought his lot over here, though his freaks were good freaks. I can still remember his Fat Lady, who was not only quite reasonably fat but both young and pretty, which of course is not in the bond. I have called her reasonably fat, for I do not think I have ever seen in any show what I would call a *really* fat lady. Elsewhere, perhaps, but not in a show.

The travelling freak-van of old had its contents concealed behind a painted canvas, covering the whole front and depicting the object within under conditions and in surroundings hardly quite realizable, one was tempted to think, within the limitations of a caravan. There mermaids combed their hair on rocks, or swam lazily about in warm tropic seas; there boa constrictors wound themselves round the bodies of paralysed Indian maidens, in the depth of Amazonian jungles. Were it a giant who lurked within, a troop of Lifeguardsmen, helmeted and plumed, rode far below his outstretched arm; while elsewhere the mighty African lion strewed the sand with the dismembered fragments of a hundred savages. All this I absorbed somewhat disconsolately, at my first St. Giles's Fair, wandering sadly down the row of painted booths; for my private means would not allow of a closer acquaintance with the interiors, and so I was obliged in imagination to swim in golden lagoons and wander through parrot-haunted jungles which I was not fated to reach in the flesh.

Perhaps after all I had the best of the bargain; for even I could not help noticing, after a while, that the audiences remained within for a remarkably short time, considering all the glories that awaited them there, and that when they came out there was on all their faces what the *Brer Rabbit* book calls "a spell ob de dry grins," showing that they had been well "spoofed " and knew it. And in fact the whole thing was unabashed "spoofery" – clumsy fakes, dried fish, abortions in bottles, mangy and sickly animals cooped in packing-cases, and so on.

There is, however, a class of spoof which is really ingenious and witty and amusing as well, and would divert an initiate just as much as those who were deceived. Sanger was a master at that sort of joyous fake, two good examples of which will be found in the tale of Madame Stevens, the Pig-faced Lady, in Chapter XV, and that of the Pipe-smoking Oyster in Chapter XXXII. The pack of ferocious wolves, too, that broke loose and tore a horse to pieces in the very heart of London was a most creditable and agreeable stunt, and Sanger was justifiably proud of it.

It is to the Cinema that much of this wholesome change in the public taste is due. Few fairs of any size are now without an excellent cinema, where we country-folk get the stuff we really like – that is, something as far removed as possible from the quiet and somewhat eventless life we lead. Nature studies and the like may appeal to a jaded London audience; we would fain be, for the fleeting moment, something rather slightly different from our daily selves – say a New York millionaire in love with an Indian half-breed; or a lovely heroine, one moment dancing a two-step in a vast and glittering hall thronged with rank and fashion, the next, without even an audible click, being swept down foaming rapids, raising an appealing, be-diamonded hand to heaven, and wearing, strangely enough, three times as much clothing as she ever appears in on dry land. We like – indeed we prefer – when we call on our stockbroker to buy a hundred Rubbers, to find him stretched out on the floor with a bowie-knife through his chest and to be ourselves arrested for the murder. We like it because it is not exactly the sort of life we daily lead; and as we stroll homeward across the starlit common towards our farmhouse, vicarage, or simple thatched cottage, we think, "I wish – Oh, how I wish – I had married an Indian half-breed!"

If in these random recollections of mine there is found more than a touch of the idyllic, little of the sort is seen in this book of Mr. Sanger's, recording as it does the facts of a strenuous life in the hardest of dry lights. Sanger was born in 1827, and was actively helping his showman-father as early as 1833, when these memoirs begin; and rural England then was as far removed from the England of today as from the Sicily of Theocritus. Though it was also the country of *Cranford* and *Our Village*, it was still the country of Fielding, where the police were a small and a feeble folk, and people continued to settle their feuds with fist and cudgel; where, too, unfortunately for the poor showman, the three orders of squire, parson, and "tough" seemed to join forces against him. The squire "lagged" or "jugged" him without much inquiry into right or wrong; the parson "barred" him, and incited his congregation to do the same; while the rough element, after a fair or a race-meeting, considered it a fitting ending to a happy day to smash up the defenceless showman and all his belongings. Of course it is just those scenes of crime and violence that would make the most vivid impression on the mind of a little boy, and doubtless there were also, in due course, idylls and spells of tranquility; but the fact remains that the first half of the book consists of a string of animated scenes both of actual and appalling crime and of most terrifying misadventure.

But the period was also the one in which Dickens was busy collecting his first impressions of that side of life, and in the early chapters his show-people leap to life again and show themselves justified in every detail. Here is a passage, for instance, from the record of 1833 (Dickens would then be twenty-one) in which the little George, aged six, was shrilly proclaiming the attractions of his father's peep-show: "'Walk up!' I would pipe, 'walk up and see the only correct views of the terrible murder of Maria Martin. They are historically accurate and true to life, depicting the death of Maria at the hands of the villa in Corder in the famous Red Barn. You will see how the ghost of Maria appeared to her mother on three successive nights at the bedside, leading to the discovery of the body and the arrest of Corder at Eveley Grove House, Brentford, seven miles from London....The arrest of the murderer Corder as he was at breakfast with the two Miss Singletons. Lee, the officer, is seen entering the door and telling Corder of the serious charge against him. Observe the horrified faces, and note also, so true to life are these pictures, that even the saucepan is shown upon the fire and the minute-glass upon the table timing the boiling of the eggs!'"

There you find the authentic note: all that wealth of small detail so beloved of Mrs. Jarley and her audiences, and told in just the same language. In Chapter XXVIII, again, is a corroboration of the exposure by Dickens in *Bleak House* of the grisly details of London burying-places.

Nothing that Dickens did in this line was truer to life than Mrs. Grudden, who is still to be found attached to many circuses, contentedly doing all the odd jobs that seem to be nobody's business in particular, and a solid line or two of her own as well.

Such a one we came across once in a little seaside town. When the weary caravans drew into their pitch late one afternoon, it was Mrs. Grudden who unharnessed the horses and led them off to water, helped everybody and directed everybody without fuss or ostentation, started the fire, washed the greens, prepared supper, and at odd moments sat at caravan steps and mended costumes. Next morning she was early in the High Street, in bonnet and shawl, with a capacious basket, doing all the marketing for the troupe. When the afternoon performance began, it was she who took our money at the box office, and when the principal item in the programme was reached at last, to wit, the Grand International Fantastic Bare-back Ballata, and the band played in the tall spotted old circus-horse, with easy amble and gentle inclination ringwards, there on his pad, to our great delight, stood Mrs. Grudden, erect, sylph-like, if a trifle bunchy in the upper quarters. As they swung round the arena, the horse and she, we were given the Nations each in turn, with the appropriate costume, dance and pantomime. The costumes she seemed to shake out of herself as a sailor shakes a reef out of a sail; in turn they were swiftly discarded and flung to earth, while such things as caps, shillelaghs, and the flag of the moment were deftly tossed up to her by the clown. As France, erect in Columbine skirt of red, white and blue and a cap of Liberty, she danced the *Carmagnole* to the music of the *Marseillaise*, and a Spanish matador, with flowing cloak and little round cap with button on top, she thrust with an imaginary rapier at a fire-breathing bull who, fortunately for us all, was not present, though even if he had been I should have felt quite safe under the regis of Mrs. Grudden. As a sailor-boy in loose blue slacks she danced an English horn-pipe and heaved at the said slacks with a will; an Irishman, pipe in hatband and breeches unbuttoned at the knees, she jigged it heel and toe; and in a twinkling was Rob Roy MacGregor, in kilt, plaid and bonnet, footing a reel, with the appropriate twirls and howls, never quitting the broad pad of her imperturbable steed. When we tore ourselves away at last, glancing towards the caravans we espied Mrs. Grudden, back in her bonnet and shawl and rusty black gown, seated on an upturned bucket, contentedly peeling spuds.

Sanger's father, the proprietor – and constructor, apparently – of the primitive peep-show of the early chapters, may fairly be considered one of the ancestors of the present Cinema in direct line. "It had twenty-six glasses, so that twenty-six persons could see the views at the same time, the pictures being pulled up and down by strings. At night it was illuminated by a row of tallow candles set between the pictures and the observer, and requiring very regular snuffing." The pictures themselves, which measured about four feet by two and a half, were painted by a (usually) intoxicated Irishman who lived in Leather Lane, his prices being for ordinary crimes (but with plenty of strong colour), three-and-sixpence; battle-pieces, where corpses were more plentiful, seven-and-six. From this to Hollywood and Los Angeles may seem a long road, but at least it is a straight one. In 1852 we find the ever up-to-date Sanger replacing his father's faithful old peep-show by one of those new-fangled magic-lanterns. The rest is modern history.

George Sanger, the genesis of whose self-bestowed title must be sought in his own entertaining pages, was quite the most famous showman of his day or perhaps of any day. He was Napoleonic in his courage, swift decisions, and power to recognize and seize opportunities; most of all, perhaps, in his evident conviction that there was no limit except actual population to the possible extension of the show-world, so that if the happy time ever arrived when we were all at last, men and beasts together, grouped under various shows and eternally displaying ourselves and our tricks to one another, he would not be more than satisfied. He brought circuses to the very doors of thousands who, but for him, might never have seen them; and possibly this very insistence of his, that you should see a circus whether you would or not, is the cause of the somewhat dulled public appetite for this form of entertainment that seems to be noticeable now. That, and perhaps the growth of the passion for games. Fifty years ago the serried masses of the football fans would to some extent have streamed into Sanger's shows. Sanger would have seen to it; he would have made them.

It is interesting to note that Sanger, who, beginning as a conjurer, had handled every possible line of show-stuff in his time, from the moment that he first took over a circus seems to have recognized the one and only profession for his powers, and never looked back, but went on from triumph to triumph till his circuses formed a planetary system all over the Continent, and in England were almost a Milky Way. He made enormous sums of money, and his elephants and camels were as the flocks and herds of the Old Testament patriarchs. Those were the palmy days of circuses. All right-minded persons went to circuses – their children took good care they did. The glaring posters covered every hoarding, on every road one met their great mysterious closed vans. Where are they all now, and – what is more interesting – what change in the public taste is causing their shrinkage in number, if not their disappearance? Possibly the dwindling employment of the horse has led to an abatement of the interest taken in him as an animal. Children nowadays much prefer a shiny motor-car to a cream-coloured Arab or a piebald pony, though no motor that I know of can stand on its hind-legs and do enchanting tricks, or lie down and pretend to be dead. Or perhaps it simply means that there is no longer a "Lord" George Sanger.

Well, if our circus-revels now are ended, which I devoutly hope is not really the case, at least their record will remain, writ by their own Prospero. For a magician George Sanger really was, sending out his Ariels along all the roads of the world, and with masques and solemn processions entertaining kings and queens – yea, ever her who gives its title to that bygone period, Queen Victoria herself. Therefore some will prefer the later chapters of this simple but high-spirited book, records of triumph upon triumph in this strange world of barbaric display and trumpeting processions wherein he moved like an emperor. For myself I like best the early struggles, the simple joys and sorrows, the wanderings of little George and his indomitable father upon the open road with its ale-houses and toll-gates, over commons, or with their pitch on a wayside strip of grass, with their peep-show and its accompanying patter. And I like to think that in one of their little roadside audiences might have been seen, lingering and listening and noting, a handsome young man, a bit of a dandy in his dress, already known to his friends as a lad of some promise – one Charles Dickens.

1925. K. G.

# INDEX

*Good roads, good times,
and merry tenting!*

*That is the showman's
benison.*